La Salle
and the Explorers of the Mississippi

WORLD EXPLORERS

La Salle
and the Explorers of the Mississippi

Tony Coulter

Introductory Essay by Michael Collins

CHELSEA HOUSE PUBLISHERS

New York · Philadelphia

On the cover Portrait: detail from *La Salle Petitions the King for Permission to Explore the Mississippi* by Howard Pyle. Courtesy of the Delaware Art Museum. Entire painting on page 73.

Chelsea House Publishers
Editor-in-Chief Remmel Nunn
Managing Editor Karyn Gullen Browne
Copy Chief Juliann Barbato
Picture Editor Adrian G. Allen
Art Director Maria Epes
Deputy Copy Chief Mark Rifkin
Assistant Art Director Noreen Romano
Series Design Loraine Machlin
Manufacturing Manager Gerald Levine
Systems Manager Lindsey Ottman
Production Manager Joseph Romano
Production Coordinator Marie Claire Cebrián

World Explorers
Senior Editor Sean Dolan

***Staff for* LA SALLE AND THE EXPLORERS OF THE MISSISSIPPI**
Copy Editor Karen Hammonds
Editorial Assistant Martin Mooney
Picture Researcher Joan Beard
Senior Designer Basia Niemczyc

3 5 7 9 8

Library of Congress Cataloging-in-Publication Data

Coulter, Tony.
La Salle and the explorers of the Mississippi / Tony Coulter.
p.   cm.—(World explorers)
Includes bibliographical references and index.
Summary: A history of the exploration of the Mississippi River, discussing the men who accomplished it.
ISBN 0-7910-1304-9
      0-7910-1527-0 (pbk.)
1. Mississippi River—Discovery and exploration—Juvenile literature.
2. Mississippi River valley—Discovery and exploration—Juvenile
literature. 3. Mississippi River valley—History—To 1803—Juvenile
literature. 4. La Salle, Robert Cavelier, Sieur de, 1643–87—
Juvenile literature. 5. Explorers—Mississippi River valley—
Biography—Juvenile literature. 6. Explorers—France—
Biography—Juvenile literature. [1. Mississippi River—Discovery
and exploration. 2. La Salle, Robert Cavelier, Sieur de, 1643–87.
3. Joliet, Louis, 1645–1700. 4. Marquette, Jacques, 1637–75.
5. Explorers.] I. Title. II. Series.   90-46198
F352.C85   1990   CIP
977'.01'092—dc20   AC

CONTENTS

WORLD EXPLORERS

THE EARLY EXPLORERS

Herodotus and the Explorers of the Classical Age
Marco Polo and the Medieval Explorers
The Viking Explorers

THE FIRST GREAT AGE OF DISCOVERY

Jacques Cartier, Samuel de Champlain, and the Explorers of Canada
Christopher Columbus and the First Voyages to the New World
From Coronado to Escalante: The Explorers of the Spanish Southwest
Hernando de Soto and the Explorers of the American South
Sir Francis Drake and the Struggle for an Ocean Empire
Vasco da Gama and the Portuguese Explorers
La Salle and the Explorers of the Mississippi
Ferdinand Magellan and the Discovery of the World Ocean
Pizarro, Orellana, and the Exploration of the Amazon
The Search for the Northwest Passage
Giovanni da Verrazano and the Explorers of the Atlantic Coast

THE SECOND GREAT AGE OF DISCOVERY

Roald Amundsen and the Quest for the South Pole
Daniel Boone and the Opening of the Ohio Country
Captain James Cook and the Explorers of the Pacific
The Explorers of Alaska
John Charles Frémont and the Great Western Reconnaissance
Alexander von Humboldt, Colossus of Exploration
Lewis and Clark and the Route to the Pacific
Alexander Mackenzie and the Explorers of Canada
Robert Peary and the Quest for the North Pole
Zebulon Pike and the Explorers of the American Southwest
John Wesley Powell and the Great Surveys of the American West
Jedediah Smith and the Mountain Men of the American West
Henry Stanley and the European Explorers of Africa
Lt. Charles Wilkes and the Great U.S. Exploring Expedition

THE THIRD GREAT AGE OF DISCOVERY

Apollo to the Moon
The Explorers of the Undersea World
The First Men in Space
The Mission to Mars and Beyond
Probing Deep Space

CHELSEA HOUSE PUBLISHERS

Into the Unknown

Michael Collins

It is difficult to define most eras in history with any precision, but not so the space age. On October 4, 1957, it burst on us with little warning when the Soviet Union launched *Sputnik,* a 184-pound cannonball that circled the globe once every 96 minutes. Less than 4 years later, the Soviets followed this first primitive satellite with the flight of Yury Gagarin, a 27-year-old fighter pilot who became the first human to orbit the earth. The Soviet Union's success prompted President John F. Kennedy to decide that the United States should "land a man on the moon and return him safely to earth" before the end of the 1960s. We now had not only a space age but a space race.

I was born in 1930, exactly the right time to allow me to participate in Project Apollo, as the U.S. lunar program came to be known. As a young man growing up, I often found myself too young to do the things I wanted—or suddenly too old, as if someone had turned a switch at midnight. But for Apollo, 1930 was the perfect year to be born, and I was very lucky. In 1966 I enjoyed circling the earth for three days, and in 1969 I flew to the moon and laughed at the sight of the tiny earth, which I could cover with my thumbnail.

How the early explorers would have loved the view from space! With one glance Christopher Columbus could have plotted his course and reassured his crew that the world was indeed round. In 90 minutes Magellan could have looked down at every port of call in the *Victoria's* three-year circumnavigation of the globe. Given a chance to map their route from orbit, Lewis and Clark could have told President Jefferson that there was no easy Northwest Passage but that a continent of exquisite diversity awaited their scrutiny.

In a physical sense, we have already gone to most places that we can. That is not to say that there are not new adventures awaiting us deep in the sea or on the red plains of Mars, but more important than reaching new places will be understanding those we have already visited. There are vital gaps in our understanding of how our planet works as an ecosystem and how our planet fits into the infinite order of the universe. The next great age may well be the age of assimilation, in which we use microscope and telescope to evaluate what we have discovered and put that knowledge to use. The adventure of being first to reach may be replaced by the satisfaction of being first to grasp. Surely that is a form of exploration as vital to our well-being, and perhaps even survival, as the distinction of being the first to explore a specific geographical area.

The explorers whose stories are told in the books of this series did not just sail perilous seas, scale rugged mountains, traverse blistering deserts, dive to the depths of the ocean, or land on the moon. Their voyages and expeditions were journeys of mind as much as of time and distance, through which they—and all of mankind—were able to reach a greater understanding of our universe. That challenge remains, for all of us. The imperative is to see, to understand, to develop knowledge that others can use, to help nurture this planet that sustains us all. Perhaps being born in 1975 will be as lucky for a new generation of explorer as being born in 1930 was for Neil Armstrong, Buzz Aldrin, and Mike Collins.

The Reader's Journey

William H. Goetzmann

This volume is one of a series that takes us with the great explorers of the ages on bold journeys over the oceans and the continents and into outer space. As we travel along with these imaginative and courageous journeyers, we share their adventures and their knowledge. We also get a glimpse of that mysterious and inextinguishable fire that burned in the breast of men such as Magellan and Columbus—the fire that has propelled all those throughout the ages who have been driven to leave behind family and friends for a voyage into the unknown.

No one has ever satisfactorily explained the urge to explore, the drive to go to the "back of beyond." It is certain that it has been present in man almost since he began walking erect and first ventured across the African savannas. Sparks from that same fire fueled the transoceanic explorers of the Ice Age, who led their people across the vast plain that formed a land bridge between Asia and North America, and the astronauts and scientists who determined that man must reach the moon.

Besides an element of adventure, all exploration involves an element of mystery. We must not confuse exploration with discovery. Exploration is a purposeful human activity—a search for something. Discovery may be the end result of that search; it may also be an accident,

as when Columbus found a whole new world while searching for the Indies. Often, the explorer may not even realize
the full significance of what he has discovered, as was the
case with Columbus. Exploration, on the other hand, is
the product of a cultural or individual curiosity; it is a
unique process that has enabled mankind to know and
understand the world's oceans, continents, and polar regions. It is at the heart of scientific thinking. One of its
most significant aspects is that it teaches people to ask the
right questions; by doing so, it forces us to reevaluate what
we think we know and understand. Thus knowledge pro-
gresses, and we are driven constantly to a new awareness
and appreciation of the universe in all its infinite variety.

The motivation for exploration is not always pure. In
his fascination with the new, man often forgets that others
have been there before him. For example, the popular
notion of the discovery of America overlooks the complex
Indian civilizations that had existed there for thousands of
years before the arrival of Europeans. Man's desire for
conquest, riches, and fame is often linked inextricably with
his quest for the unknown, but a story that touches so
closely on the human essence must of necessity treat war
as well as peace, avarice with generosity, both pride and
humility, frailty and greatness. The story of exploration is
above all a story of humanity and of man's understanding
of his place in the universe.

The WORLD EXPLORERS series has been divided into four
sections. The first treats the explorers of the ancient world,
the Viking explorers of the 9th through the 11th centuries,
and Marco Polo and the medieval explorers. The rest of
the series is divided into three great ages of exploration.
The first is the era of Columbus and Magellan: the period
spanning the 15th and 16th centuries, which saw the discovery and exploration of the New World and the world
ocean. The second might be called the age of science and
imperialism, the era made possible by the scientific ad-
vances of the 17th century, which witnessed the discovery

of the world's last two undiscovered continents, Australia and Antarctica, the mapping of all the continents and oceans, and the establishment of colonies all over the world. The third great age refers to the most ambitious quests of the 20th century—the probing of space and of the ocean's depths.

As we reach out into the darkness of outer space and other galaxies, we come to better understand how our ancestors confronted *oecumene*, or the vast earthly unknown. We learn once again the meaning of an unknown 18th-century sea captain's advice to navigators:

> And if by chance you make a landfall on the shores of another sea in a far country inhabited by savages and barbarians, remember you this: the greatest danger and the surest hope lies not with fires and arrows but in the quicksilver hearts of men.

At its core, exploration is a series of moral dramas. But it is these dramas, involving new lands, new people, and exotic ecosystems of staggering beauty, that make the explorers' stories not only moral tales but also some of the greatest adventure stories ever recorded. They represent the process of learning in its most expansive and vivid forms. We see that real life, past and present, transcends even the adventures of the starship *Enterprise*.

The Father of Waters

"The Father of Waters again goes unvexed to the sea." So wrote Abraham Lincoln, 16th president of the United States, in a telegram dated August 26, 1863. The reference was to an event that had taken place some seven weeks earlier—the surrender of the Confederate fort at Vicksburg, Mississippi, to Union forces commanded by Ulysses S. Grant. Possessed of an appreciation for military strategy nearly as great as his gift for writing elegant prose, Lincoln recognized that the fall of the Mississippi stronghold, which overlooked a bend in the great river, was an all but critical loss for the Confederacy. With Vicksburg in Grant's hands, the Mississippi was now free to Union navigation for almost its entire length (New Orleans had fallen earlier), thus hastening the inevitable collapse of the Southern economy. Not even the great Union victory at Gettysburg, Pennsylvania, which occurred almost simultaneous to Vicksburg's capitulation and halted the farthest northern penetration of the gray-coated Confederate forces, loomed as large in Lincoln's consciousness. With Vicksburg's fall, Lincoln, who had guided the Union through its darkest hours, was for the first time able to see the way clear to victory.

It is not surprising that at the moment of greatest crisis for the young American republic, the man who had been entrusted with its survival should have his gaze firmly fixed on the Mississippi, for it has always occupied a central

René-Robert Cavelier, Sieur de La Salle, glances over his shoulder at a map of the North American regions he explored. La Salle was the first to understand the vast strategic importance of the Mississippi as the gateway to the North American interior.

place in the American consciousness. North America's greatest waterway, the figurative dividing line between the "civilized" East and the wide open spaces of the West, it flows some 2,348 miles from its source in Lake Itasca in Clearwater County, Minnesota, to the Gulf of Mexico, some 80 miles south of New Orleans, Louisiana. Ten states border on it; with the Missouri, which joins it at St. Louis, Missouri, it forms the third largest river system in the world, behind only the Nile and the Amazon. Spanning almost the entire north-south breadth of the United States, it is also the traditional gateway to the West and well deserves the affectionate paternal appellation by which Lincoln referred to it, for it mixes its waters with more than 100 tributaries, among them the Ohio, the Illinois, the Arkansas, and the Missouri. Throughout much of the history of the United States, the Mississippi has been a pathway to settlement, the country's most important interior waterway, and its most valuable commercial highway.

But Lincoln's words notwithstanding, the Father of Waters has seldom gone unvexed on its tortuous way to the sea. Eons ago, seismic upheavals and glacial movements helped determine the future course of the river; more recently, the river has done its own work. Flooding often alters its sinuous course, swallowing up islands and shoreline, altering the region's geography through the deposit of some of the several million tons of sediment it carries each year to the Gulf. Heedless of man's directives, the river simply carves its own course. For example, the great American writer Samuel Clemens—who grew up on the Mississippi's shore; who piloted the famous steamboats that plied its waters during much of the 19th century; who took his pen name, Mark Twain, from a depth measurement frequently called out by riverboat pilots; and whose greatest fictional works, most notably *Huckleberry Finn*, are set on the river—estimated that between 1699 and 1850 the river eliminated almost 200 miles of its length in its

The Great Lakes and Mississippi River region. La Salle claimed this entire region for France, although bad luck, political intrigue, betrayal, and his own problematic character prevented him from successfully establishing colonies there.

The Great Lakes and
the Mississippi River

CANADA

NORTH
DAKOTA

MINNESOTA

SOUTH
DAKOTA

WISCONSIN

Lake Superior

L. Nipissing

Sault. Ste. Marie

St. Ignace

French R.

Ottawa R.

Lake Huron

Georgian Bay

MICHIGAN

Mississippi R.

St. Francis Xavier

L. Ontario

NEW
YORK

IOWA

NEBRASKA

Fox R.

Lake Michigan

Lake Erie

Ft. St. Joseph

PENNSYLVANIA

OHIO

MD.

Ft. St. Louis

Illinois R.

Ft. Crevecouer

INDIANA

WEST
VIRGINIA

ILLINOIS

Missouri R.

KANSAS

MISSOURI

Ohio R.

KENTUCKY

VIRGINIA

Arkansas R.

OKLAHOMA

ARKANSAS

Ft. Prudhomme

TENNESSEE

NORTH CAROLINA

SOUTH
CAROLINA

River

MISSISSIPPI

Mississippi

LOUISIANA

ALABAMA

GEORGIA

FLORIDA

GULF OF MEXICO

TEXAS

lower valley, as the region of lakes, bayous, oxbow curves, islands, and magnolia, palmetto, and cypress trees between the Gulf of Mexico and its confluence with the Ohio River is known.

For the many Indian tribes that made their homes along or near the river, including the Ojibwa, the Fox, the Sauk, the Quapaw, the Chickasaw, the Choctaw, the Natchez, the Huron, the Sioux, and the Winnebago, the river was a frequent battlefield, a cause of warfare among themselves and against the white newcomers who sought to trade and settle there. There, too, Winnebojo, the hero of much of the mythology of the Indians of the upper valley, performed his epic feats in the days before humans walked

El Adelantado Hernando de Soto.

The Spanish conquistador Hernando de Soto is generally credited with being the first European to discover the Mississippi. He supposedly gazed at its waters from a promontory somewhere near present-day Chickasaw Bluffs, Mississippi, in 1541.

the earth—slaying the water lynx who caused the waters to overflow their bounds, tricking and then vanquishing the great serpents, defeating the giants, removing the mammoth boulders that impeded the river's progress.

But after the arrival of the first whites in the upper Mississippi valley, Winnebojo seemed to lose much of his power. The Spanish conquistador Hernando de Soto is generally given credit for the European discovery of the Mississippi, which he apparently reached somewhere near present-day Chickasaw Bluffs, Mississippi, in 1541, but Europeans had been fascinated by stories of the great river almost from the moment that they set foot in the New World, and a map drawn by Christopher Columbus as early as 1507 indicates the mouth of the Mississippi. The Spanish, after de Soto, called the Mississippi the Rio Grande de Florida (the Great River of Florida, which for the Spanish constituted much of the southeastern United States), but they proved more interested in the gold and silver to be found to the south and the west than with the immense river that splits the heart of the continent.

Spain's inattention proved France's opportunity. The first important French voyages to the New World were made by the Breton mariner Jacques Cartier in the 1530s. Cartier, like most of the first European voyagers to the Americas, was actually searching for a westward route to the Indies and China, but he discovered instead the Gulf of St. Lawrence and the St. Lawrence River. Although Cartier's own attempts at colonization failed, the St. Lawrence valley became the locus of later French colonization efforts. Between 1605 and 1635, the French explorer Samuel de Champlain founded settlements on Nova Scotia and at Quebec, and by the time of his death in 1635, French fur traders—the legendary *voyageurs* and *coureurs du bois*—had roamed as far west through the great North American woodlands as Wisconsin. In the process, they had helped give France claims to the interior of the continent; they also brought back reports of a tremendous river the Indians called the Mechesebe. Apparently, according to the Indians, this waterway was so long that no man had yet traveled its length. Some said it flowed south for its entire course and emptied into the Gulf of Mexico; others that it veered west and rolled to the Vermillion Sea, the Gulf of California, or the South Sea, as the Pacific Ocean was alternately referred to at the time.

In either case, a generation of French explorers found such reports tremendously exciting, for with thick forest blanketing almost the entire eastern part of the continent, rivers were the easiest way to explore the vast interior. The old dream of a waterway west to the Indies still lived; if the Mississippi indeed flowed west to the Pacific, and if a link between it and the great lakes that the French had discovered to the southwest of the St. Lawrence could be found, the French would find themselves possessors of the Northwest Passage, which had so long been sought after by the nations of Europe as a route to the wealth of Asia. If it flowed south, it would still provide France with the opportunity to establish its own trading posts near Mexico and hem in Spain before its European rival could expand its holdings in the region. Should the river connect with the Great Lakes and by extension with the St. Lawrence, the French would have claims to a massive North American empire and a water link between its most far-flung outposts. The French government therefore saw the Mississippi, if it could be found, as possessing vast strategic advantages; French trading companies and individual fur traders viewed the unexplored regions as a likely source of pelts and lucrative new contacts with the Indians; French clerics saw in the no doubt "heathen" inhabitants of the region new opportunities to win souls for Catholicism. But of all the men whose lives would become intertwined with the "fatal river" that rolled "like a destiny, through its realms of solitude and shade," as Henri Joutel described it, none would play a greater role than René-Robert Cavelier, Sieur de La Salle.

This late-17th-century Spanish map of the Mississippi River contains imaginative renderings of Lake Superior and Lake Michigan (labeled here as Lago de los Ilinois). One of La Salle's forts has been drawn in on the Illinois River (R Ilinois) just southwest of Lago de los Ilinois. The annotation in the lower right-hand corner indicates that the map was based on La Salle's journeys.

Early Years and First Expedition

René-Robert Cavelier, known later as La Salle, was born in Rouen, France, a city on the Seine River some 70 miles northwest of Paris, on November 21, 1643. The second son of Jean Cavelier and Catherine Geest, he grew up in an environment dominated by business and religion. His father, Jean, was a successful wholesale merchant, and many of René-Robert's relatives on both sides of the family were prosperous businessmen. Young René-Robert was initially tutored at home, but by the age of nine he had begun attending a local grammar school run by the Jesuits, as the clergymen of the Catholic missionary order the Society of Jesus are known. It was apt training for a future explorer, for in the little more than a century since their founding, the Jesuits had already established a reputation for their willingness to carry the Gospel to the most remote regions of the globe. Young Cavelier apparently flourished under the Jesuits, for just short of his 15th birthday, he moved to the great city of Paris to enter a Jesuit novitiate.

After taking his preliminary vows of devotion to the order in 1660, Cavelier enrolled at the Collège Henri IV, a Jesuit educational institution in La Flèche, near Angers. There he began his "philosophy," a three-year course in logic, physics, metaphysics, and mathematics. Because so many of its lay students were young noblemen preparing for careers in the army or navy, Collège Henri IV was one of the best places in France to obtain an education in geography, astronomy, and navigational science, all of which

This 17th-century map is more noteworthy for its depiction of the flora, fauna, and native inhabitants of New France than it is for geographic accuracy. The cartographer has correctly portrayed the French colony as a sparsely settled, vast region covered with thick forest and inhabited by a variety of Indian tribes and unusual animals— porcupines, wolves, foxes, and marten—but his placement of the territory's waterways is flawed.

La Salle as a young man. As a youth, according to his biographer Francis Parkman, "he showed an inclination for the exact sciences, and especially for the mathematics," but "his calm exterior hid an inexhaustible fund of pride."

were then considered branches of mathematics. The many Jesuit graduates who became missionaries in little-known territories must also, however, have appreciated such practical training. It was probably this adventurous aspect of the religious life that most appealed to Cavelier, who was good at his subjects, particularly mathematics, but was also, as his superiors noted, restless by nature.

After finishing his philosophical studies at La Flèche, Cavelier spent a couple of years teaching at Jesuit grammar schools in Tours and Blois. It was customary for young Jesuit professors to teach for four or five years before resuming their studies in theology, the completion of which qualified them for ordination as a priest and for missionary work. But Cavelier's impatience to undertake a foreign mission soon became so intense that he took the highly unorthodox step of writing directly to Father Oliva, superior general of the Society of Jesus, requesting that he be released from some of his normal obligations. He had his mind set on becoming a missionary in China, where Jesuit astronomers had been welcomed at the emperor's court, as he related in a letter written to Oliva on March 28, 1666:

> For eight full years, which is ever since my entrance into the Society, I have been desiring and petitioning with the greatest eagerness for admission to China. . . . I have a very good training in mathematics. I have, too, a ready and retentive memory for languages. . . . I am large and robust of body and in particular am capable to a high degree of enduring heat and cold. . . . So now, as I have reached my twenty-third year . . . and am teaching grammar for the third year, I most humbly plead with your Very Reverend Paternity to deign either to send me thither, there to become a priest, or else to put me at theology . . . so that I may arrive [at China] the sooner.

Characteristically impatient, several days later, on April 5, Cavelier wrote a second letter suggesting that he be allowed to take a teaching position in Portugal, which was a jumping-off spot for Jesuit missionaries on their way to the Far East. Oliva denied both of the eager young novitiate's requests, but he did permit him to begin his theological training immediately. Cavelier returned to La Flèche, where for a time his work seems to have satisfied him, but his restlessness soon returned. On December 1, 1666, he wrote Oliva again, requesting once more to be sent to Portugal to finish his studies. This time, Oliva advised patience and ordered Cavelier to "[r]emain quietly in your province until you have finished your studies, . . . after which I will try to give effect to your desire, which is quite full of genuine zeal."

This latest setback proved too much for Cavelier, who throughout his life would display a limited capacity for frustration and a noticeable determination to heed only

The Jesuit college at La Flèche, where La Salle received his religious training. After his break with the order, he was to become its implacable enemy, and he often accused the Jesuits—sometimes correctly—of undermining his plans.

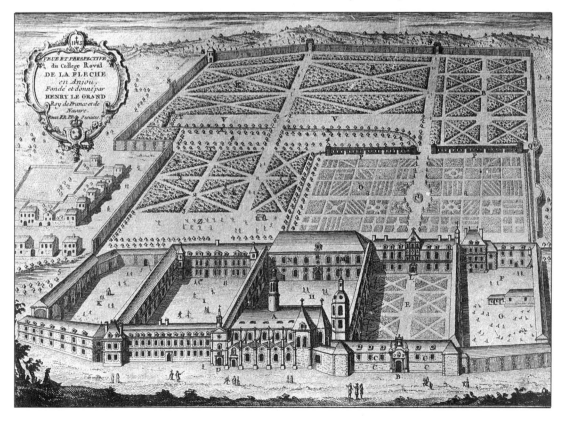

a Citadelle . . . . . | 6. Les Iesuittes . . . . | QUEBEC | 11. Riviere de S. Charles | 16. Haute Ville . . .
e Chasteau . . . . . | 7. N. Dame Cathedrale . | Capitale de la Nouvelle | 12. l'Hospital general . . | 17. Basse Ville . . . .
Magasin aux Poudres. | 8. Le Palais . . . . | France, Evesché — | 13. Hermitage des Recolets | 18. Plate forme et baterie de Can
es Recolets . . | 9. Le Seminaire . . . | et Siege de Court | 14. l'Evesché . . . . | 19. Isle d'Orleans . .

The city of Quebec, which became the capital of the royal province of New France in 1663, is built upon a huge rock that towers some 300 feet above the St. Lawrence River. It was founded in 1608 by Samuel de Champlain upon a site that the French explorer Jacques Cartier first visited in 1535.

the dictates of his own counsel. It may also have marked the beginning of the animosity toward the Jesuits that he would display for the rest of his days. At the start of the new year, he requested permission to leave the society. His release was granted him in March of 1667, and suddenly, after nine long years of studying to become a priest, he found himself free to make his own plans. His father had died some years earlier, but because of the vow of poverty Cavelier had taken on entering the novitiate, he had not been able to accept the inheritance that would normally have been his. Neither his brother Nicholas nor his sister, who together controlled the family funds, were willing to grant him anything more than a small yearly allowance, which meant that he was now in urgent need of finding some suitable occupation.

The Cavelier family, and indeed Rouen in general, had many links to New France, as France's settlements in Canada were known. René-Robert's uncle, Henri Cavelier, had been involved in the founding of Montreal as a member of a group of shareholders known as the Hundred Associates. More recently, his cousin Jacques Le Ber had emigrated to Montreal, where he had become a prosperous merchant. Only a year before, René-Robert's older brother Jean, a Sulpician priest, had also gone to Montreal, to become a missionary. It was thus only natural that René-Robert's family should advise him to look toward Canada as the ideal place to begin a new life. His uncle's name would be well known and well respected there, and his brother and cousin would be able to help him get established. René-Robert saw the logic of these arguments, and early in the summer of 1667 he set sail for Canada.

Two recent developments made it a good time to settle in Montreal. In 1663, King Louis XIV had declared that New France was from then on to be considered a French province. Previously, the right to develop French territories in the New World had been granted by the Crown to various chartered companies, including the Hundred Associates. After the king's edict, the companies gave way to an administration directed from France by Jean-Baptiste Colbert, Louis's new minister of the marine. A royal governor in Quebec was made responsible for relations with the French government and for the defense of the colony. An intendant, also based in Quebec, was given charge of the colonial economy, judicial system, and police. Trois-Rivières and Montreal, the only places in New France, besides Quebec, with sizable populations, were both given deputy governors of their own.

The second important development was that by the autumn of 1666 the powerful Iroquois Confederacy, which

had come close to annihilating the colony, had been effectively contained. The confederacy was an alliance of
five Indian nations—the Mohawk, Oneida, Onondaga,
Cayuga, and Seneca—that had been at war not only with
the French but with the Algonquian Indians as well. It
controlled much of present-day New York State and Pennsylvania, and its warriors claimed hegemony over the St.
Lawrence Valley and even as far west as the Mississippi.
The Algonquians, who were allied with the French, consisted of many nations, including the Shawnee, Ottawa,
Delaware, Potawatomi, and Chippewa. Conflict between
the French, the Iroquois Confederacy, and the Algonquian tribes revolved around the fur trade, which was the
main source of income for the colony and essential for
the survival of the Indians. The Algonquians wished to
trade directly with New France, which infuriated the Iroquois, who considered the Algonquians their vassals and
wished to control the fur trade themselves. Fearsome warriors, the Iroquois had hated the French since a series of
defeats handed them by Champlain much earlier in the
century. Therefore, aligning themselves with the Dutch
and the English, the Iroquois had periodically harassed
France's colonists until their decisive defeat by the French
forced them to sue for peace.

Now that the Iroquois had been at least temporarily
subdued and the charter companies restrained, the Sulpician religious order, which in 1663 had been granted
ownership of Montreal—characterized by the historian
Francis Parkman as then being "perhaps the most dangerous place in Canada" on account of the enmity of the
Iroquois—began to step up their efforts to attract settlers.
René-Robert Cavelier, the brother of one of these Sulpicians and the cousin of a respected local merchant, must
have seemed to them an ideal person to help further their
plans. At any rate, shortly after Cavelier arrived in Montreal, the Sulpicians gave him a large tract of land on the
south shore of the island; he in turn agreed to recruit

settlers from France to live on this property. After rounding up a crew of laborers, Cavelier moved onto his land and carved out from the heavy forest the boundaries of a village he named Côte de St. Sulpice. To complete his transformation from failed Jesuit to seigneurial landlord, he decided to elevate himself to the minor nobility. Without having the technical right to do so, he began calling himself "de la Salle," taking his name from a family property near Rouen called La Salle.

At St. Sulpice, La Salle, as he was now widely known, farmed and traded for furs. Ideally situated up the St. Lawrence from Montreal, he bartered extensively with the local Indians and soon grew quite prosperous. La Salle was, however, temperamentally unsuited for such a settled life, and he was soon to trade it away for something infinitely more dangerous and uncertain. Already, people marked qualities in him that set him apart: a certain restlessness that drew upon a sturdy, well-developed frame and significant reserves of stamina; a quiet, withdrawn manner that La Salle attributed to intense shyness and his enemies chalked up to arrogance; a solemn manner that his friends characterized as dignified and his enemies as sullen; a love of the wilderness that owed much to his apparent discomfort with human society; a scrupulous discretion, almost chasteness, regarding personal behavior. Although La Salle was rugged enough, as he would prove, to handle just about anything that the wilderness could throw at him, he had little sympathy for the libertinism practiced by many of his rough-and-tumble contemporaries, and he was apparently a very difficult man to get to know. Like many who have struggled to fulfill a personal vision, La Salle really trusted only himself. This natural diffidence, coupled with his strict views of acceptable personal deportment, possibly a vestige of his religious training, would earn him many enemies. But those few who did understand him, such as his friends the Sieur de La Forest and Henri de Tonti, remained intensely devoted

Jean-Baptiste Colbert was one of King Louis XIV's most able ministers. Under his direction, France's industry and commerce were reorganized. A firm believer in the development of overseas colonies to strengthen France's home economy, Colbert was instrumental in convincing the king to take control of New France away from the chartered fur trading companies and make it a royal province.

and had no hesitation proclaiming La Salle, as did Tonti, "one of the greatest men of this age, a man of an admirable spirit."

One fall day in 1668 a group of Seneca Indians appeared on La Salle's property. He allowed them to winter at St. Sulpice, and they told him of a great river called "Ohio." It flowed, they said, toward the west, passed through country rich in buffalo, and eventually emptied itself into the sea. The river could be reached by means of a three-day journey from their homes, which lay in the territory to the south of Lakes Ontario and Erie. On hearing this, La Salle wondered whether this might not be the same river the Spanish called Colorado, which supposedly had its source somewhere in the Northeast and emptied into the Vermillion Sea. And if the Ohio and the Colorado were one and the same, might this river not be the long-sought passage to China?

This illustration from a 1664 history of Canada depicts the deaths of the seven French Jesuit missionaries to the Iroquois known collectively as the North American martyrs. The engraving shows the deaths of these missionaries as occurring simultaneously when in fact they occurred thoughout the late 1640s at different locations. Of all the northeastern Indian tribes, the Iroquois were the most resistant to French influence.

La Salle soon became obsessed with the idea of finding the Ohio and the route to China. His enthusiasm must have been sufficiently strong that it overcame his customary taciturnity, for he apparently talked about his dreams frequently enough to spur one of the local wits to sarcastically dub his estate La Chine (China), a nickname that has survived until this day. (It was not the first La Chine in the region. More than a century earlier, another French seeker of China, Jacques Cartier, had ventured up the St. Lawrence until the great rapids beyond Montreal halted his quest. Equally obsessed with China, Cartier named the falls that halted his search La Chine.) Somewhat bored with his life at La Chine, La Salle began making plans for an expedition to the Ohio. His Seneca guests would serve La Salle as guides, but finding money to implement his scheme presented a more difficult problem. In order to raise the capital necessary to fund such an undertaking—expenses would include the hiring of a crew of experienced voyageurs and the purchase of a large supply of trade goods for exchange with the Indians en route—La Salle sold part of his estate back to the Sulpicians in November 1668. The rest of his holdings, including his home and several other buildings, he sold to an ironmonger less than one month later.

Sometime early in 1669, La Salle traveled to Quebec in order to ask Governor Courcelles for permission to search for the Ohio, to explore along its banks, to engage in trade along the way, and, ultimately, to look for a passage to the western sea. Courcelles quickly approved of La Salle's plans but requested that La Salle team up with two Sulpician priests, the Abbés Barthélemy and François Dollier de Casson, who were about to set off in search of a river they called Mississippi. The clerics had learned of the river from an Indian prisoner who originally belonged to a tribe that lived somewhere to the southwest. This Indian, who was probably a Shawnee, had told of many unknown tribes living along the banks of the Mississippi.

La Salle's rude dwelling at La Chine, as the estate granted to him by the Sulpician fathers of Montreal came to be known. From La Chine, he made several excursions into the north woods for the purpose of studying the Indians, and during his years there he mastered eight Indian dialects.

The Sulpicians wished to discover these peoples so that they might convert them to Christianity. It seemed to the governor that La Salle and the two priests were probably interested in the same territory, that Ohio and Mississippi might even be two different names for the same river or two different branches of one body of water. If such were the case, the two expeditions might as well pool their resources, Courcelles reasoned. With his training in navigation and mapmaking, La Salle would be able to help the Sulpicians with any geographic problems that might arise.

Some time after this agreement was reached, Abbé de Queylus, the Sulpician superior, began to have doubts about the expedition. He feared that La Salle, about whose character he harbored suspicions, might abandon the priests. For that reason, he asked Abbé Barthélemy to remain at home and in his place substituted Deacon René de Brehaut de Galinée. Galinée, an experienced surveyor, later published a detailed account of the journey La Salle and the others were about to embark on. (Many French priests, particularly Jesuits, could draw on a richness of wilderness experience comparable to that of any voyageur. Using the fur traders' route, which avoided Iroquois country by taking them west from the St. Lawrence via the Ottawa River, by portage to Lake Nipissing, and ever westward on the waters of the French River to the Georgian Bay, the hardy Jesuits established missions on Manitoulin Island; at Michilimackinac, the strait where Lake Huron connects with Lake Michigan; at Sault Ste. Marie, where Lake Huron flows into Lake Superior; at the southern end of Green Bay; and even, for a time, at the western end of Lake Superior. These fearless Jesuits were therefore often prime sources of geographic information, which they gleaned from their travels and their Indian converts, but their preeminence in the region would prove to be a source of discontent for La Salle.)

On July 6, 1669, La Salle and the Sulpicians finally began their expedition. From the shores of Lake St. Louis, at a point near La Salle's former property, they paddled slowly up the St. Lawrence River in the direction of Lake Ontario. The French party consisted of seven canoes, each carrying three men. Ahead of this column floated two more canoes, bearing the Seneca Indians who had agreed to act as guides. The boats the Frenchmen traveled in had been made by Algonquian Indians and were of the type most frequently used by Canadian traders and missionaries. So light that they could easily be carried by one man, these canoes, of birchbark construction, could nevertheless carry 4 men and up to 900 pounds of supplies.

At first, La Salle and his companions traveled only with great difficulty, as rapids and rocks often made it necessary for them to carry or drag their boats. The river became more easily navigable, however, after they reached a point near present-day Ogdensburg, New York. At the end of

The bill of sale for La Salle's land and buildings at La Chine, which he sold in 1668 in order to raise funds for a proposed expedition in search of the Ohio River, the existence of which he learned about from the Iroquois.

each long day of paddling they went ashore to seek shelter and food. In his narrative, Galinée described their typical meal:

> The ordinary diet is Indian corn . . . which is ground between two stones and boiled with water; the seasoning is with meat or fish, when you have any. This way of living seemed to us all so extraordinary that we felt the effects of it. Not one of us was exempt from some illness before we were a hundred leagues from Montreal.

After enduring many miseries, on August 2, La Salle and the Sulpicians at last reached Lake Ontario, which, Galinée wrote, came into sight "like a great sea." On the 11th of August they landed on the south side of the lake, at Irondequoit Bay, just north of the present-day city of Rochester, where they were approached by a number of Seneca as soon as they disembarked. The Indians offered them presents and then escorted them to the largest of a group of 4 Seneca villages that lay some 18 to 20 miles inland. This settlement, Gandachiragoo, stood on top of a small hill, in the middle of a clearing about 5 miles in circumference, and consisted of a cluster of about 150 bark houses surrounded by a primitive stockade. As soon as La Salle and the others had climbed the hill, they were greeted by a group of old men, the village elders, who welcomed them and offered food and shelter.

On the following day, 50 or 60 of the most important members of the tribe gathered in the Frenchmen's lodgings. As presents were being exchanged, the Frenchmen declared that they came on behalf of Onontio (as the Seneca called the governor) in search of the Ohio River and the Shawnee Indians living near it. They asked to be given a slave captured from that nation, who might act as their guide and lead them to Shawnee territory. The Seneca agreed to provide them with such a guide but told the French they would have to wait until a group of villagers, who had taken all the slaves with them, returned from trading with the Dutch.

La Salle and the others spent an uneasy week waiting for the return of the trading party, during which time they endured the death threats directed toward them by the relatives of a Seneca who had been murdered in Montreal. The explorers, however, remained vigilant and escaped any harm. During this same period several warriors returned to the village with a prisoner, who seemed to belong to the tribe the Sulpicians were searching for, but the Indians were not willing to offer this man to the French to serve as a guide. They planned instead to sacrifice him in order to appease the relatives of a warrior who had been killed.

This map of New France drawn in 1673–74 by Louis Jolliet, who discovered the Mississippi for France, gives some indication of the French conception of the geography of the massive continent they were seeking to tame. Note that Jolliet has drawn trees all over his map; at the time virtually the entire eastern portion of North America was covered by thick forest.

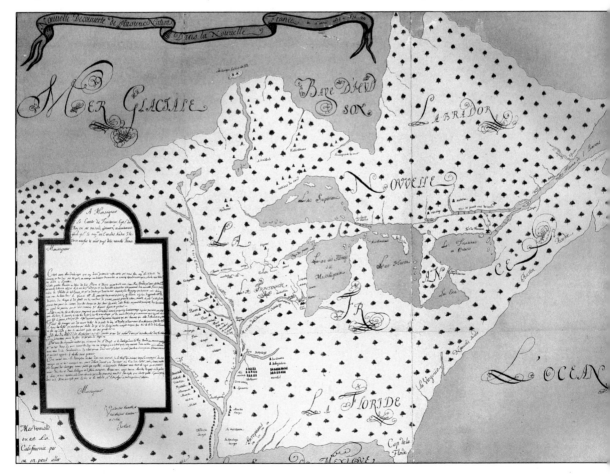

As the Seneca prepared for the execution of their prisoner, many of the Indians in the village seemed to be growing dangerously frenzied. It seemed to La Salle that his party might now be in peril, and he persuaded the others that it would be wise to move some distance away from the village. Several of the men, however, did not wish to miss the execution and stayed behind. They reported the next day that the prisoner had been tortured for hours before being killed with a stone. His body had then been torn to pieces, cooked, and eaten.

Days passed, but the Seneca still did not produce a guide. They excused themselves by saying that the trading party had not yet returned, but it was becoming increasingly obvious that they had no real desire to help the Frenchmen, and for good reason: Because of their dominance of the eastern Great Lakes region, the Iroquois functioned as middlemen, trading both with the tribes of the interior and with Canadian merchants. To give the French direct access to the Shawnee and other western tribes would therefore be to cut themselves out of the trade chain. Accordingly, they tried to convince the French that it would be foolish to travel to the territory they wished to see, because the Indians there were bloodthirsty and would surely kill them. At other times, they maintained that the only route to the Ohio involved a portage of about 180 miles, which for the purposes of La Salle and future trading parties was impracticable.

The impasse came to an end with the arrival at the French camp of an Iroquois from another village, which was called Tinawatawa. In this village, the Indian said, there were a number of slaves taken from the tribes the French were looking for, and his people would be glad to give the French several of them to serve as guides. Since Tinawatawa lay to the west, in the direction of Lake Erie, La Salle decided to let the Indian lead the French party to his home.

On September 24, after traveling to the southern end

of Lake Ontario, the French arrived at the Iroquois village. It stood some 15 miles inland, at a spot slightly north of present-day Hamilton, Ontario. The inhabitants received them kindly and gave them two slaves captured from the Ottawa. These captives seemed quite willing to act as guides and assured the explorers that the Ohio could be reached in six weeks.

To their great surprise, La Salle and the others learned that two Frenchmen had arrived at Tinawatawa a day before them. One of these was Adrien Jolliet, who was returning from the southern shores of Lake Superior, where he had been searching for copper. The Ottawa Indians living in that area had given him an Iroquois prisoner as a gesture of amity toward the Five Nations, with whom they wished to conclude a peace. This Indian told Jolliet of a method, previously unknown to the French, of traveling from Ottawa to Iroquois country. Guided by the Iroquois, Jolliet had returned east by way of Lake Huron, the St. Clair River, Lake Erie, and, after leaving Tinawatawa, the portage around Niagara Falls.

Besides informing them of this new route, Jolliet also told La Salle and the Sulpicians about an Algonquian tribe he had heard of, the Potawatomi, who lived near "the great river that leads to the Shawnee." This tribe was very populous and had never been evangelized. On hearing this, the two Sulpicians, Dollier and Gallinée, both of whom were fluent in Ottowan, one of the major branches of the Algonquian language group, decided to reverse Jolliet's route and continue their search for the Ohio by passing through Algonquian rather than Iroquois territory.

For reasons of his own, which have been much speculated upon, La Salle did not wish to follow the clergymen. Complaining of sickness, which Gallinée, in his account, sarcastically attributed to his fright upon encountering a trio of rattlesnakes sunning themselves upon a rock, he informed the Sulpicians of his desire to return to Montreal. No one knows for certain what his intentions were, but it seems likely that he was bent on pursuing the course of action he had outlined for Governor Courcelles. Although still a devout Catholic, he was more concerned with glory for himself and a wilderness empire for France than new souls for the Sulpicians. He had, moreover, since his days as a novitiate, cultivated an intense dislike for the Jesuits, whose missionaries had already established themselves in the regions Jolliet spoke of and whose presence there was enough to convince La Salle to go elsewhere. (La Salle believed, as did many others, that the Jesuits were as concerned with obtaining political power as they were with their spiritual duties. He accused them, among other things, of being eager to establish missions so that they could use their influence over the local Indians to control and profit from the fur trade.) But as Abbé de Queylus had feared, La Salle, whatever his reasoning, was now leaving the priests to fend for themselves. The clerics, however, would soon prove themselves supremely capable of surviving on their own.

On September 30, 1669, the expedition split into two groups. La Salle and his men headed east, while the Sulpicians and their party set off toward the west. Leaving Tinawatawa behind them, Dollier and Galinée wintered in a log cabin on Lake Erie, where they said mass daily and supped well on the bountiful game they were able to shoot. After reaching the far end of the lake, they crossed through the straits at present-day Detroit and into Lake Huron, then paddled northward, hugging the northwestern shores of Huron until, on May 25, 1670, they reached Sault Ste. Marie and a tiny Jesuit mission, consisting of a stockade, chapel, and house rudely constructed from logs hewn out of the thick forest nearby. From the two Jesuit priests stationed there, Jacques Marquette and Claude Dablon, they learned that a mission to the Potawatomi had already been established the preceding autumn by Father Jean-Claude Allouez, another Jesuit. Disappointed, after three days of Jesuit hospitality the Sulpicians decided to return to Montreal. With the aid of a French guide lent them by the Jesuits, Gallinée and Dollier made the return voyage by the traditional French route of the French River to Lake Nipissing to the Ottawa to the St. Lawrence.

As for La Salle, no one knows for sure how he spent the winter of 1669–70. It is certain that he did not return to Montreal, and there are no records of his movements until the summer of 1670, when the fur trader Nicolas Perrot met him near the Ottawa River. Some historians, citing documents attributed to La Salle, hold that after leaving the Sulpicians he indeed found his way to the Ohio, which he descended as far as the falls at present-day Louisville, a claim that even his contemporary and great rival, the fur trader and explorer Louis Jolliet (Adrien's brother), saw fit to credit. Many modern scholars are less certain, however, and believe that there is little evidence to support La Salle's contention. It is more likely, they assert, that he spent the winter of 1669–70 in the wild trading among the Iroquois, collecting furs, honing his wilderness skills, and increasing his knowledge of Indian life.

An artist's rendition of a French priest at an Indian village in the wilderness. Many French clergymen—Sulpicians, Jesuits, Franciscans—roamed the wild as fearlessly as any voyageur, and by the 1660s, French missions stretched from the St. Lawrence Valley as far west as Lake Superior.

The Mississippi Rediscovered

When Dollier and Galinée arrived in Montreal in June 1670, they brought with them news of a "great River called by the Iroquois, Ohio, and the Outawacs, Mississippi . . . [whose] ordinary course was from East to West." Many questions remained unanswered about this waterway, but it was vital that it not fall into the hands of the Spanish or English, since it might well provide a route to the interior of the continent or perhaps even a passage to China.

Intendant Talon therefore decided to commission a new expedition to seek out the Mississippi, and his choice to lead that expedition was La Salle. In his report to Colbert, Talon simply states, without mentioning the expedition of the previous year, that La Salle "had the right temperament for these enterprises." In any event, sometime in the fall of 1670, Talon summoned La Salle to Quebec and commissioned him to go toward the "South West and South," taking possession of whatever country he passed through. After reaching the "Messi-Sippi" by way of the Wisconsin River, he was to travel downstream in search of a "passage to Mexico."

Whether or not La Salle actually engaged in any voyages of exploration after receiving this commission has been a subject of controversy. Some 19th-century historians believed that La Salle did in fact locate the Mississippi sometime between 1670 and 1672, but the explorer himself

Father Jacques Marquette, the redoubtable Jesuit who accompanied Jolliet on his expedition to the Mississippi. This priestly explorer spoke six Indian languages and had a keen interest in geography.

never claimed any such thing, and it has been convincingly demonstrated that this is almost certainly not true. Little is known about La Salle's movements between October 1670 and December 1672, but most likely he spent those two years trading with Indians in the wild. Certainly, by the time of his later expeditions, he demonstrated a knowledge of the languages and customs of the various Indian tribes that bespoke of long periods spent among them.

In the summer of 1672, Talon received word that one year earlier an English expedition had crossed the Appalachian Mountains and reached the Kanawha River, which flowed down their western side. At about the same time that the English were crossing the mountains, Talon had taken steps to claim the Great Lakes for France. With the representatives of 14 tribes in attendance at Sault Ste. Marie, the soldier of fortune Simón François Daumont, Sieur de Saint-Lusson, accompanied by Perrot, Louis Jolliet, and the Jesuits Dablon and Allouez, formally claimed the region "in the name of the Most High, Mighty, and Redoubted Monarch, Louis, Fourteenth." But still fearing that the English might beat the French to the Mississippi, and having heard nothing from La Salle in two years, the intendant began to cast about for someone else to send in search of the river. His choice was the 27-year-old Jolliet.

A first-generation Canadian, Louis Jolliet was born at Beauport, near Quebec, in September of 1645. The second son of Marie d'Abancourt and a wheel maker named Jehan Jollyet, young Louis grew up surrounded by people deeply committed to the development of New France, among them Seigneur de Beauport and the widow of Jean Nicolet, the pious discoverer of Lake Michigan and Green Bay.

Jolliet lost his father before his sixth birthday. When his mother married a wealthy merchant named Godefroi Guillot, the family moved to Quebec, where at the age of 10 Jolliet was enrolled in a Jesuit college. Louis excelled in music, free drawing, mapmaking, and mathematics, and for several years he planned to become a priest. When he was 17 he took his preliminary religious vows, but in 1667 he left the Jesuits, finding himself unsuited for the monastic life. After spending the winter of 1667 in France, Jolliet on returning to Quebec set about preparing himself to take up the fur trade. In the summer of 1668, having purchased trade goods, he set out for Sault Ste. Marie to look for furs. He spent much of the next three years in the wilderness.

Talon had several reasons for selecting Jolliet to carry out the task La Salle had failed to perform. Not only was the intendant already acquainted with Adrien Jolliet, whom he had dispatched to Sault Ste. Marie in search of copper deposits, but he had previously had occasion to admire the younger Jolliet's intellectual abilities after engaging him in theological debate at the seminary several years earlier. Jolliet had ample experience in the wilderness, and his success as a fur trader demonstrated a practical side that La Salle, for one, seemed to lack.

This early map of Lake Huron also charts currents and depth measurements. At the upper left is the strait that the Indians called Michilimackinac, which connects Lake Huron and Lake Michigan; on its shores the Jesuits established the mission of St. Ignace. The mapmaker has drawn a score of boats in that region because it was such a popular fishing spot for the Indians.

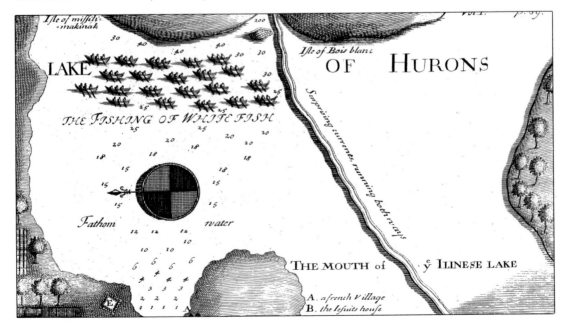

Selected to travel with Jolliet was Father Jacques Marquette, a 35-year-old Jesuit with a passion for geography whom Dollier and Gallinée, the wandering Sulpicians, had met at Sault Ste. Marie. Marquette had also served at the mission of St. Esprit, at the western end of Lake Superior, where Hurons and Ottawas had fled to escape the ravages of the Iroquois, and after the Sioux drove him back east, at St. Ignace at Michilimackinac. Fluent in several Indian languages, Marquette had long desired to proselytize among the nations living along the Mississippi.

In December 1672, the two men met at St. Ignace, which Jolliet had reached after a three-month solo journey from Quebec along the usual route. After spending the winter at the mission, the priest and the fur trader, accompanied by five others, departed on May 17, paddling westward in two canoes across the upper reaches of Lake Michigan. Although many historians credit the Jesuit with being the leader of the expedition, Jolliet, not Marquette, was in command. Likewise, the sole primary account of the voyage, traditionally attributed to Marquette, was probably not penned by him. It is now thought to have been written by Dablon, the Jesuit superior in the Great Lakes region, from Marquette's notes and Jolliet's journal.

Whoever its leader and scribe, the Jolliet and Marquette expedition arrived at St. Francis Xavier mission, located at the southern end of Green Bay not far from what is now De Pere, Wisconsin, near the end of May. From there, they ascended the Fox River to a Mascouten village in the vicinity of present-day Berlin, Wisconsin. At the time, this village marked the western boundary of French exploration. The Mascouten, Dablon wrote, "could not sufficiently express their astonishment at the sight of seven Frenchmen, alone and in two canoes, daring to undertake so extraordinary and so hazardous an expedition." The Indians supplied the explorers with two guides and informed them that by ascending the Fox River they would

In the winter of 1669, Father Marquette, who was then stationed at the mission of the Holy Spirit at Lake Superior's Chequemegon Bay, promised his superior in a letter that "if the Savages who promise to make me a Canoe do not break their word to me, we shall explore this River [the Mississippi] as far as we can."

find "a portage of half a league beyond which was another river which came from the northwest."

According to Dablon, Jolliet's party left the Mascouten village at the beginning of June "to enter countries wherein no European had ever set foot." The Mascouten guides showed the Frenchmen the way up the Fox River to the portage, and the explorers then carried their canoes and luggage overland to the banks of the Wisconsin. Arriving at a spot near present-day Portage, they then descended some 118 miles to the mouth of the river, which they reached on June 15.

There, the Wisconsin fed into a great river that the Frenchmen immediately recognized as the Mississippi, the "Father of Waters" that had so long been sought. Dablon described the scene that met their eyes:

> [The Mississippi] is narrow at the place where Miskous [the Indian name for the Wisconsin] empties; its Current, which flows southward, is slow and gentle. To the right is a large Chain of very high Mountains, and to the left are beautiful lands; in various Places, the Stream is Divided by Islands. On sounding, we found ten brasses [fathoms] of Water. Its Width is very unequal; sometimes it is three-quarters of a league, and sometimes it narrows to three arpents [a French unit of measurement slightly smaller than an acre].

As they proceeded down the Mississippi, which Marquette christened "Rivière de la Conception" (River of the Immaculate Conception, then a disputed theological doctrine much embraced by the Jesuits) and Jolliet dubbed the Buade, after the new governor of New France, the Frenchmen observed a great deal of wildlife, including several large herds of buffalo. The country through which they traveled was, however, empty of any signs of human habitation. The explorers, Dablon wrote,

> continued to advance, but, As we knew not whither we were going,—for we had proceeded over one Hundred

A Huron couple. The Huron lived to the north and west of the French settlements in the St. Lawrence Valley and were willing trade partners with the French, but their role as the middlemen in the fur trade infuriated their traditional enemy, the ferocious Iroquois.

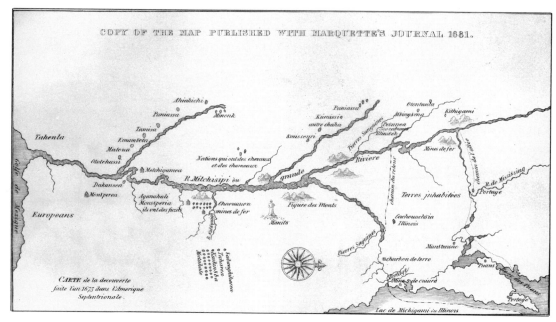

COPY OF THE MAP PUBLISHED WITH MARQUETTE'S JOURNAL 1681.

This map of the Mississippi illustrated an edition of Marquette's alleged journal that was published in 1681. It is oriented differently than most maps; south is at left, north at right.

leagues without discovering anything except animals and birds,—we kept well on our guard. On this account, we made only a small fire on land, toward evening, to cook our meals; and, after supper, we remove Ourselves as far from it as possible, and pass the night in our Canoes, which we anchor in the river at some distance from the shore.

Finally, on June 25, the Frenchmen discovered human tracks along the water's edge, and a narrow path leading away from the river. Ordering the others to remain behind with the canoes, Jolliet and Marquette set off alone along the trail. According to Dablon, the two men remembered that they

> silently followed The narrow path, and, after walking About 2 leagues, We discovered a village on the bank of a river, and two others on a Hill distant about half a league from the first. Then we Heartily commended ourselves to God, and, after imploring his aid, we went farther without being perceived, and approached so near that we could even hear the savages talking. We therefore Decided that it

was time to reveal ourselves. This We did by Shouting
with all Our energy, and stopped, without advancing any
farther.

Jolliet and Marquette had arrived at a large Peoria Indian
village, located a few miles up the Iowa River, a western
tributary of the Mississippi. The village consisted of 300
cabins housing several thousand people. On hearing the
shouts, a crowd of Indians emerged from their cabins, and
from this group four old men stepped forward. They approached the Frenchmen, carrying two tobacco pipes, or
calumets, "finely ornamented and Adorned with various
feathers." As these elders slowly advanced, they "raised
their pipes towards the sun, seemingly offering them to it
to smoke,—without, however, saying a word." Recognizing this ceremony for what it was—a friendly overture—
the Frenchmen were reassured. They gladly took the peace
pipes that were offered them and followed the elders into
the village.

The Peoria, who belonged to the Illinois confederacy,
were, as Jolliet told Dablon, "affable and obliging and
received the explorers well. They gave in present a calumet
of about three feet long adorned with feathers of various
kinds, which was to serve them as a safeguard in their
journey." Concerning their customs, Jolliet remembered
that

> the women were very modest, and that when they did
> wrong [i.e., were unfaithful], their noses were cut off.
> Women and old men till the soil, and after sowing time,
> all go together to hunt buffaloes. The meat supply them
> with food; and the hides are made into garments after
> tanning them with a certain kind of earth, which they also
> use as [war] paint.

The explorers were also impressed by the large wooden
canoes used by the Indians, which were 50 feet long and
3 feet wide and could carry 30 men with all their baggage.
The Indians feasted their guests on fish, corn, and buffalo,

Huron men and women; an illustration from an early French history of Canada. The Huron economy quickly became dependent on trade goods that it obtained from the French, which is why French traders and missionaries were generally welcome in Huron territory. The Huron and other western tribes also hoped to gain French protection from the Iroquois.

showered them with gifts, and probably also loaned them the services of a guide.

Sometime near the end of June, Jolliet, Marquette, and the others left the Peoria village and continued their descent of the Mississippi. Nothing more is known about their voyage until they passed below the mouth of the Illinois River. Somewhere between the Illinois and the mouth of the Missouri the explorers paddled beneath petroglyphs, or rock paintings, which deeply impressed them. As Dablon reported:

> While Skirting some rocks, which by Their height and Length inspired awe, We saw upon one of them two painted monsters which at first made Us afraid. . . . They are as large As a calf; they have Horns on their heads Like those of deer, a horrible look, red eyes, a beard Like a tiger's, a face somewhat like a man's, a body Covered with scales, and so Long A tail that it winds all around the Body, passing above the head and going back between the legs, ending in a Fish's tail. Green, red, and black are the three Colors composing the Picture. Moreover, these 2 monsters are so well painted that we cannot believe that any savage is their author; for good painters in france would find it difficult to paint so well.

Leaving this frightening apparition behind them, the travelers pressed on. They passed the mouths of the Missouri and Ohio without much incident. Around July 25, some 40 days after entering the Mississippi, they spotted a settlement on the water's edge. Located just above the mouth of the Arkansas River, this was Quapaw, one of four Arkansas villages in the area.

As the Frenchmen drew closer, a crowd of hostile Indian warriors quickly formed along the river's edge. Dablon reports what happened next:

> They were armed with bows, arrows, hatchets, clubs and shields. They prepared to attack us, on both land and water; part of them embarked in great wooden canoes— some to ascend, others to descend the river, in order to

Intercept us and surround us on all sides. Those who were on land came and went, as if to commence The attack. In fact, some Young men threw themselves into The water, to come and seize [our] Canoe[s]; but the current compelled Them to return to land. One of them hurled his club, which passed over us without striking us. In vain I showed The calumet, and made them signs that we were not coming to war against them. The alarm continued, and they were already preparing to pierce us with arrows from all sides, when God suddenly touched the hearts of the old men, who were standing at the water's edge. This no doubt happened through the sight of our Calumet, which they had not clearly distinguished from afar; but as I did not cease displaying it, they were influenced by it, and checked the ardor of their Young men. Two of these elders even,—after casting into our canoe, as if at our feet, Their bows and quivers, to reassure us—entered the canoe, and made us approach the shore, whereon we landed, not without fear on our part. At first, we had to speak by signs, because none of them understood the six languages which I [Marquette] spoke. At last we found an old man who could speak a little Illinois.

At night, Jolliet and Marquette and the other members of the expedition pulled their canoes up on the banks of the Mississippi to prepare dinner and sleep.

Despite this frightening welcome, the Frenchmen spent several days in the village, where they feasted on fish and a kind of corn meal known as sagamité. For the most part, the Indians treated their uninvited visitors well, but at a secret council convened by the village elders one night, several tribesmen proposed killing the strangers and robbing them of their possessions. Only the intervention of the chief of the village prevented this mayhem. After summoning the explorers, the peace-loving chief "danced the calumet dance before us . . . , and in order to banish all fear, made me [Marquette] a present of the calumet."

Upon inquiring about the distance to the sea, Jolliet and Marquette were told it could be reached in 10 days. Actually, as they were still more than 700 miles away from the Gulf of Mexico, it would have taken them closer to 4 weeks at the rate they were traveling. Nevertheless, despite their perceived proximity to the river's outlet, the Frenchmen decided to turn back. "After attentively considering that we were not far from the gulf of Mexico," Dablon reports, "we judged that . . . beyond a doubt, the Mississippi river discharges into the florida or Mexican gulf, and not to the east in Virginia, . . . or to the west in California." Furthermore, Jolliet and Marquette worried that

This depiction of Marquette's journey down the Mississippi was painted by Frederic Remington, the late-19th-century American artist who won fame for his Western scenes. Marquette and Jolliet enjoyed a remarkably peaceful passage on the great river.

if they advanced any farther, they would be trespassing on
the Spanish territory of Florida, thereby exposing themselves and their companions to the danger of capture. They
also feared that they would be unable to resist "Savages
allied to The Europeans, who were numerous, and expert
in firing guns, and who [they had been told by the Ar-
kansas] continually infested the lower part of the river."
Although the explorers were disappointed that the Mississippi apparently emptied into the Gulf of Mexico and not
the "Sea of the South," they consoled themselves by pos-
tulating that one of the Mississippi's western tributaries
might provide the long-sought route to China. On about
July 25, the Frenchmen left the Arkansas village and began
their return voyage.

Little is known about the trip back to the Great Lakes
except that the explorers utilized an alternate route. Instead
of remaining on the Mississippi until its confluence with
the Wisconsin, Marquette and Jolliet left the great river
at its juncture with the Illinois. It is not known how the
explorers learned of this shortcut to the Great Lakes. They
may have heard of it from Father Allouez, who had met
them at St. Francis Xavier at the start of their expedition,
or perhaps an Indian clued them in. However they learned
of the new route, as they paddled up the Illinois, which
Jolliet dubbed the St. Louis, toward Lake Michigan, Jolliet
found himself enormously impressed by the attractiveness
of the Illinois River valley. Dablon reports him as observ-
ing that the valley

> seemed to me the most beautiful and suitable for
> settlement. At the place where we entered the lake is a
> harbor, very convenient for receiving ships. . . . This river
> is wide and deep, abounding in catfish and sturgeon. For a
> distance of eighty leagues, not a quarter of an hour passed
> without my seeing game . . . . Oxen, cows, stags, does
> and turkeys are found there in much greater number than
> elsewhere. There are [wide] prairies . . . [and] forests of
> the same extent. . . . A settler would not have to spend

Immortalized in stone, a watchful Jolliet gazes into the distance from the back of his steed. In life, however, this explorer and wilderness entrepreneur was more often conveyed by a canoe or his own two legs than by a horse.

ten years in cutting and burning trees; on the very day of his arrival he could put his plow into the ground. . . . After sowing grains of all kinds, a settler could devote himself to planting vine, and grafting fruit-trees; to tanning ox-hides, wherewith to make shoes, and with the wool of these oxen [i.e., buffaloes], he could make finer cloth than that brought here from France. Thus he would easily find in the country his food and clothing, and nothing would be wanting.

About 200 miles up the Illinois, Jolliet and Marquette arrived at a Kaskaskia Indian village of about 75 cabins, where they were treated kindly and supplied with a guide. After leaving the village, the Frenchmen ascended the Illinois to its junction with the Des Plaines, then continued up the latter river to the Chicago portage. From Chicago they went up to the west shore of Lake Michigan, then on to St. Francis Xavier, where they arrived toward the middle of October. After having traveled more than 4,000 miles in 5 months, their expedition was finally complete.

After several weeks of rest, Jolliet continued on to Quebec, which he reached after a harrowing journey on which he lost many of his maps and documents concerning the Mississippi and almost his life. Marquette, who had reached Green Bay seriously ill, remained at St. Francis Xavier, but in the spring of 1675 he felt well enough to return to the Kaskaskia village on the Illinois, where he established a new mission, the Immaculate Conception of the Blessed Virgin. Feeling his health waning, he attempted to return to St. Ignace but perished short of his goal, on the eastern shore of Lake Michigan, near present-day Ludington. According to those who were with him, on his deathbed Marquette thanked God for allowing him to die poor and in the wilderness, like his beloved Saint Francis Xavier, the Jesuit monk revered as the apostle to the Indies. Both Catholic and Indian legend associate miraculous healings with Marquette's burial place, but his undeniable legacy, shared with Jolliet (who lived 25 more years, most of it spent in the Canadian wilderness), is the discovery of America's greatest river.

This allegorical representation of the explorers of the Mississippi bringing the blessings of European civilization to the region's native inhabitants adorns the state capitol in St. Paul, Minnesota. At left, a Marquette figure extends the cross toward the Indians, while at right, a dashing La Salle figure, with flowing sable tresses, approaches.

Heartbreak in the Valley

While Jolliet and Marquette were making their discoveries, important developments were also taking place in the life of La Salle. By the time La Salle resurfaced in 1673, Governor Courcelles had been recalled to France and had been replaced by Louis de Buade, Comte de Frontenac and de Palluau. This profligate nobleman, the godson of Louis XIV, had been exiled to Canada because of a cavalier disregard for paying his debts that was reckless even by the dissolute standards of the French aristocracy. But Frontenac was always able to make the best of an opportunity, and in the New World he soon came to share La Salle's dream of a western empire in the interior of the continent. He also became La Salle's all-important patron and protector and was one of the few people with whom the reticent La Salle was able to reach a true understanding.

Shortly after taking office Frontenac decided to build a fort at Cataraqui, on the north shore of Lake Ontario near present-day Kingston. His purpose was ostensibly to cut off trade between the Iroquois and other Indians and the Dutch and English at Albany, but the governor also realized that whoever controlled such a stronghold could profit enormously by acting as a middleman in the trade between the French colony and the Indians. In order that his plans not be thwarted, Frontenac decided to finance the fort privately and to erect it without first receiving official approval.

A kneeling La Salle presents his petition concerning colonization and trading schemes in New France to the Sun King, Louis XIV, in 1675. An observer at the French court described La Salle as "a man of great intelligence and sense. He rarely speaks of any subject except when questioned about it, and his words are very few and precise."

One of the people to whom Frontenac turned for financing was Jacques Le Ber, the wealthy Montreal merchant. Because Le Ber was La Salle's cousin, it was probably through him that Frontenac became acquainted with La Salle. The governor was seeking "some person of credit" whom he could send among the Iroquois "to advise them of his intentions." Deciding that La Salle was "a person qualified for such a service by the different journeys he had made into that country and by his acquaintance with the Indians," Frontenac chose the explorer as his emissary to the Iroquois.

La Salle carried out his mission to the governor's satisfaction, and once the fort, which was named after Frontenac, had been built he traveled widely among the Iroquois telling them where to bring their furs. At first, things proceeded according to plan, but when the authorities in Paris got wind of the illegal trading activities going on at Fort Frontenac they immediately tried to put a stop to them. In the spring of 1674, Colbert, who was by now Louis's controller general of finances, ordered Frontenac to halt the unauthorized commerce. Moreover, the minister refused categorically to cover the debts that Frontenac had incurred in building his stockade and trading post.

The governor was now in a difficult situation. If his fur trade was ended, he would not be able to pay off his debts. In the meantime, La Salle had become a business partner and even closer associate of the governor's since siding with Frontenac in a power struggle with François-Marie Perot, the governor of Montreal. La Salle now proposed that he should assume all of the governor's debt and take financial responsibility for operating Fort Frontenac. In exchange, the governor would help persuade the king to grant La Salle the fort and some adjoining land. In November 1674, armed with a letter from Frontenac to Colbert in which the governor described him as "a man of intelligence and ability, the most competent of anyone I know here to accomplish every enterprise and discovery which may be entrusted to him, as he has the most perfect knowledge of the state of the country," La Salle set sail for France. His lobbying efforts proved wildly successful: On May 13, 1675, Louis awarded him the ownership of Fort Frontenac and its adjoining territory. Furthermore, "to make it known how near to our heart is the increase of the colonies in the said country" and "in consideration of the cares and expenses which the said Cavelier has borne and will bear hereafter," the king elevated La Salle to the nobility. At the age of 32, La Salle finally had the right to the title he had assumed long ago.

La Salle took control of Fort Frontenac in September 1675. Using the fort as his base of operations, he soon began trading heavily over a large area. Although the conditions of his seigneury only allowed for local commerce, La Salle enjoyed Frontenac's protection and soon began to trade over a larger area and to make enormous profits. Shortly, however, an opportunity to make even better money presented itself.

A primitive blueprint for the fortress Governor Frontenac had constructed at the northeastern end of Lake Ontario, at the spot the Indians called Cataraqui. After La Salle's reconstruction, Fort Frontenac consisted of a wooden stockade reinforced with stone ramparts, a barracks, officers' lodgings, a jail, a forge, a well, a mill, and a bakery. It was defended by 9 cannons and a permanent garrison of about 15 soldiers; its canoe men were said to be the best in America.

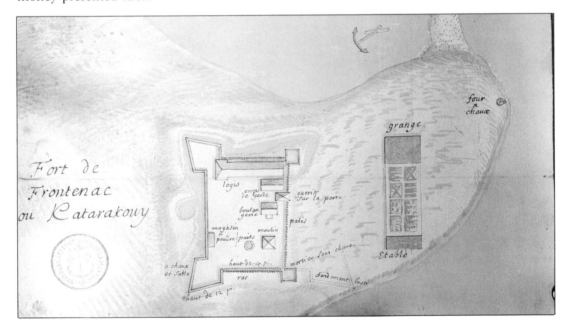

Sometime late in 1676, Louis Jolliet requested royal permission to develop the Illinois Valley, which had so impressed him with its richness and promise. Louis XIV, whose opinions on colonial expansion had recently changed, refused Jolliet's petition because he now found it "far more worthwhile to occupy a smaller area and have it well populated than to spread out and have several feeble colonies which could easily be destroyed by all manner of accidents."

Despite Jolliet's failure to win royal approval for his project, Frontenac and La Salle now began thinking of trying to establish themselves in the valley. They reasoned that if they could expand their fur-trading operations into this enormous region to the west, they would outflank any

If this portrait is an accurate likeness, La Salle grew somewhat stout and dandified as he aged, despite his years in the forest. The handwriting at bottom is his actual signature.

potential competitors and gain control of a huge commercial empire. Accordingly, they petitioned the king,
hoping, by using a different tactic, to succeed where Jolliet
had not. Rather than request permission to colonize the
Illinois Valley, they asked instead, in La Salle's name, for
approval to search for the mouth of the Mississippi. They
also applied for the right to build forts along the route,
under the same conditions applying at Fort Frontenac.

On September 7, 1677, La Salle set off once again for
France, to seek support for his scheme at the French court.
In Paris he made the acquaintance of several well-placed
lobbyists, who agreed, for a sizable fee, to represent La
Salle's case to the king. In early May 1678, Louis granted
La Salle's requests, on the condition that the expedition
be completed within five years, that it be financed at La
Salle's own expense, and that no trading be conducted
with the Indians who customarily brought their furs to
Montreal. Louis also granted him a monopoly on buffalo
hides. To finance the expedition, La Salle borrowed heavily from relatives and moneylenders, using his commission
from Louis to obtain credit. This cash he used to purchase
provisions and the services of 32 men, who accompanied
him when he left the port city of La Rochelle for New
France in July 1678. Among them was the man who was
soon to become his most able and trusted lieutenant, 28-
year-old Henri de Tonti, a Neapolitan by birth and
Frenchman by allegiance who had already enjoyed a spec-
tacular career as a naval and cavalry officer. Perhaps the
most striking feature of Tonti's rather picturesque appear-
ance was an iron claw that substituted for a right hand
blown off by a grenade in a campaign against the Spanish
in Sicily. He sometimes cloaked this metallic prosthesis
in a kind of velvet glove.

By mid-September, La Salle was in Quebec, where he
made final preparations. He spent that winter on the Niagara River, near Buffalo, where, under Tonti's supervision, his men constructed a 45-ton sailing vessel, which

The Italian-born adventurer Henri de Tonti was La Salle's ablest and most reliable lieutenant. He was the son of the Italian revolutionary and banker who developed the famous tontine system of life insurance. La Salle described Tonti as being of "honorable character and amiable disposition" and said that "his energy and address make him equal to anything."

their commander named the *Griffin* after the mythical winged beast on Frontenac's coat of arms, a likeness of which decorated the prow. In August 1679, after receiving the sacrament at a mass said by Father Louis Hennepin, a Belgian priest much enamored of exploration whom La Salle had befriended on his first visit to France and brought back to North America with him, La Salle and his men embarked. Over several weeks' time they sailed the vessel the length of Lakes Erie and Huron and, after a brief stop at St. Ignace, where La Salle heard mass cloaked magnificently in a mantle of scarlet rimmed with gold, on to Green Bay. There, after the *Griffin's* hold was filled with pelts of beaver, otter, and deer, La Salle sent the ship back to Niagara, under the command of the Danish pilot he had recruited, where it was to discharge its cargo and then return to Michilimackinac. If all went according to order, Tonti, with a party of about 20 men that La Salle had sent ahead the previous winter with instructions to gather furs, would meet the *Griffin* there, and the reunited band, aboard the ship, would meet La Salle and his group of 14 men at the mouth of the St. Joseph River.

But for La Salle, things seldom went as planned. At length, Tonti finally arrived at the St. Joseph, but there was no sign of the *Griffin*. Already, evidence of serious dissension among the men had become apparent. Several had threatened mutiny at the prospect of having to spend the winter waiting for Tonti, and at St. Ignace, La Salle had learned that a number of members of an advance group that he had sent out had deserted, taking with them provisions, furs, and trade goods. La Salle attributed their treachery to calumnies spread by the Jesuits and Montreal merchants, both of whom had good reason to resent his commission to explore in the West, but it is as likely that the discontent was bred by La Salle's single-minded and stern leadership style. Even Hennepin, who was a La Salle supporter, conceded that his friend "never took any one's advice."

With winter fast approaching, La Salle decided to move on before the St. Joseph iced over. His party now numbered 34 men, a somewhat motley assortment of voyageurs, soldiers, artisans, priests, and even a few Indians. The season's first snows had begun to fall, and the trees in the dark, barren woods were icy and bare as the band, in eight canoes, floated southwest down the St. Joseph. Deep forest alternated with plains and marshes on either side of the waterway; everywhere, the men saw the skeletons of dead buffalo, but nary a live animal for killing. As their hunger increased, so did their anger with La Salle, but serious incident was averted, for the moment, by the discovery of a buffalo bull trapped in a bog. It took 12 men, hauling on a strong rope, to drag the bellowing beast

This woodcut of industrious beavers at work at Niagara below the great falls illustrated a 1715 geography of North America. At Niagara, La Salle's men lived in bark wigwams while they constructed the Griffin.

The **Cataract** of **NIAGARA**, some make this *Water-Fall* to be half a *League* while others reckon it no more than a hundred *Fathom.*

from the ooze, but for a time the party ate well, and a semblance of good cheer returned. The Kankakee was reached, and then the Illinois, which flowed past sweeping prairies, on the edges of which, late at night, they could see campfires burning. Wooded islands loomed into view, then went past; high bluffs, topped with giant trees, towered overhead.

Around Christmastime, the voyagers arrived at a large Indian village of about 460 lodges located on a promontory known as Starved Rock. The inhabitants—Illinois Indians—were off on their winter hunt, so the Frenchmen and their companions helped themselves to some corn and moved on. Some miles downriver, at the site of present-day Peoria, La Salle and his party came upon another Illinois village. After a tense initial confrontation, both sides displayed the calumet, and an understanding was reached. La Salle informed the Indians that he had come to trade with them and to protect them against their enemy, the Iroquois. If they so wished, he would build a fort upon that spot, to which the Indians could bring furs to trade for items they desired. If they did not wish him to stay, he would move on and conduct his business with the Osage, leaving the Illinois to fend for themselves against the Iroquois. Unsurprisingly, the Indians accepted the French "offer," but matters became tense after the arrival at the village of a Mascouten chief, who in a secret nocturnal powwow sought to convince the Illinois that La Salle, as he claimed to have been told by some other Frenchmen, was a spy in league with the Iroquois, sent to deliver the Illinois to their enemies. Only a rare display of eloquence by La Salle managed to preserve the harmony between the French and their hosts.

But some of La Salle's own group were less convinced. While still suspicious of La Salle, the Illinois chief had told the French wild, fantastic tales of the horrors to be found on the Mississippi—giant lizards and serpents, raging whirlpools, evil spirits and demons—in an attempt to

A 17th-century French drawing of Iroquois warriors (lower left) along with canoes, dwellings, and some of the animals of North America. The military power of the Iroquois nation was one of the major factors in determining France's policy in North America.

frighten them away. The stories worked on some of the more credulous members of the party, and six of them, including the two most talented carpenters, decamped. Some others, unable to convince their leader to turn around, poisoned his dinner, but La Salle recovered, with the aid of an emetic he had brought for just such a contingency.

Undeterred, La Salle set his men to constructing a fortress on a hill near the Illinois encampment. Ravines on 2 sides and the river guarded the approach, and an earthen embankment and a stockade of pointed logs, 25 feet high, seemed to make the position impregnable. Perhaps in reference to the anguish he felt at the betrayal of his men, La Salle named the fortress Crèvecœur, which means heartbreak. There, the weary explorers waited out the remainder of winter.

At the beginning of March 1680, La Salle could hold out no longer. Despite the continued bitterness of the weather, he was anxious to return to Fort Frontenac, where he planned to obtain new provisions and, he hoped, ascertain the whereabouts of the *Griffin*. Taking with him 5 men and 2 canoes, La Salle left 16 men behind at Fort Crèvecœur under the command of Tonti. A couple of weeks' travel in the stinging March cold brought him to the small stockade he had left on the St. Joseph, where some voyageurs from Michilimackinac told him that there had been no sign of the *Griffin*. The first European trade ship to ply the Great Lakes was never heard from again. Indian tradition holds that it was ambushed and burned by the Iroquois, while the most recent scholarship suggests that it went to the bottom in a gale.

There was even worse news ahead. La Salle and his companions crossed the swollen St. Joseph on a raft, blazed their own trail through the frosty woods of southern Michigan on foot, followed the Huron River to Lake Erie, traversed the Detroit River on another raft, and tramped eastward through the icy rain along the flooded north shore of Lake Erie to the French fortress at Niagara Falls, only to be told that another ship, carrying a consignment of supplies sent from France for La Salle's use, had sunk at the mouth of the St. Lawrence. Several weeks' more hard traveling brought La Salle to Fort Frontenac, on May 6. He had covered 1,000 miles, much of it through largely unexplored terrain, under the most discouraging of conditions. A letter from Tonti awaited him.

Shortly after La Salle had left, his correspondent informed him, "most of his men had mutinied, wrecked Fort Crèvecœur, torn down its palisade, pillaged its storehouse, thrown into the river all arms and ammunition—save those they could carry away—and fled." Only five men, two of them priests, remained. Deeply in debt, his affairs in ruins, La Salle made plans to return to the West.

If the motivating force of La Salle's character was simple greed, as his detractors through the centuries have consistently alleged, he demonstrated an extremely poor ability to satisfy his longings. He was temperamentally unsuited for business, and his letters repeatedly display an impatience with the compromises and frustrations one must endure to achieve financial success. Again and again in his correspondence, La Salle is forced to explain why he cannot repay his debts. Certainly, if he was interested only in wealth and the comforts it buys, he could have contented himself with remaining at Fort Frontenac, where business was lucrative. But La Salle's character was more complicated. La Salle coveted riches, but he wished for glory as well, and he dreamed of much more than the countinghouse and the ledger. Indeed, he was so indifferent to the mundane details of commerce that he confessed in a letter to a financial backer (hardly the person to whom a shrewd businessman would make such an admission) that "I have neither the habit nor the inclination to keep books, nor have I anybody with me who knows how." It should be remembered that many of those contemporaries who criticized La Salle were would-be com-

A crowd of Indians gathers to watch as La Salle's men put the finishing touches on the Griffin; the illustration is from a sketch by Father Louis Hennepin. The Iroquois immediately recognized that the great ship would give La Salle an advantage in controlling the Great Lakes fur trade, and they were constantly threatening to burn it.

petitors who were angry because his ambition thwarted theirs. The desire for riches and fame was a common motivation for most of the great explorers of La Salle's epoch, but like many of them, La Salle also possessed an even grander vision. He dreamed not only of wealth— enough money, say, to live comfortably back at Montreal, or even to buy a country estate in France—but of empire: trading posts, fortresses, and settlements stretching all the way from New Canada to the Gulf of Mexico and westward beyond the Great Lakes, French dominion over the incomparable North American wilderness that was his true home. It was this vision, and his single-minded devotion to it, that made La Salle so incomprehensible to his fellow man. La Salle seemed to have no need of those niceties that even the hardiest of his fellows required occasional recourse to—wife, family, a home to which he could sometimes return. After he sold La Chine, he never again lived in any one place for any period of time, and virtually all of his time was spent in the wilderness, under conditions that would test anyone's endurance. He never married and seems to have had few, if any, amorous interests; privation and cold were his constant companions.

In the early summer of 1680, La Salle returned to the Great Lakes region, accompanied by 25 men and his great friend François Daupin, Sieur de la Forest. Most of this company, which included carpenters, masons, and soldiers, was left at Michilimackinac while La Salle, with 10 Frenchmen, 2 Indians, and an unspecified number of dogs, pushed on to the St. Joseph, the Kankakee, and the Illinois.

The Illinois country, when La Salle reached it, resembled death's playground. Charred ruins, littered with corpses, many of which had been preyed upon by wolves and carrion birds, marked the locations of the Illinois villages he had earlier visited. At deserted, demolished Fort Crèvecœur and the nearby Indian settlement, he found the burned bodies of women and children still tied to

A late-16th-century French traveler in North America did this drawing of an Indian village and customs, including a war dance (lower left), the dance of the calumet (center), and a council of elders (lower right). A calumet is at top; La Salle made frequent use of the calumet to demonstrate his peaceful intentions to the Indian tribes he encountered on his expeditions.

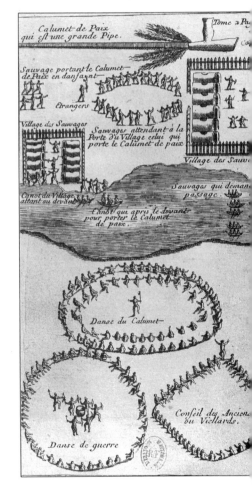

The 19th-century American artist George Catlin, noted for his portrayals of the way of life of the American Indians, also painted a series of pictures depicting La Salle's exploits. This one shows La Salle crossing a frozen Lake Michigan in the course of his epic trek to the St. Joseph River in the winter of 1680.

stakes. There was no trace of Tonti and his few remaining loyal men. The Iroquois had visited the Illinois country and made a mockery of the French claims to supremacy. Engulfed in melancholy, La Salle moved on to the mouth of the Illinois, where at last he beheld the mighty Mississippi, but he had no heart to continue on. He returned to the Illinois village, where he and his men spent a solemn early winter. One night, as La Salle brooded on the destruction and Tonti's possible fate, a comet blazed its spectral way through the heavens, adding a further note of isolation and unreality to the scene before him.

With the new year approaching, La Salle and his four companions (the others had been left behind at the fort on the St. Joseph) set out for a rendezvous with La Forest. La Salle himself described the taxing overland journey:

> Snow fell in extraordinary qualities all day, and it kept on falling for 19 days in succession, with cold so severe that I never knew so hard a winter, even in Canada. We were obliged to cross 40 leagues of open country, where we could hardly find wood to warm us at evening, and could

get no bark whatever to make a hut, so that we had to spend the night exposed to the furious winds which blow over these plains. I never suffered so much from cold, or had more trouble in getting forward, for the snow was so light, resting suspended as it were among the tall grass, that we could not use snow-shoes. Sometimes it was waist-deep; and as I walked before my men, as usual, to encourage them by breaking the path, I often had much ado, although I am rather tall, to lift my legs above the drifts.

Hungry and fatigued, La Salle and his men at last arrived at the St. Joseph, where he was relieved to find that La Forest had strengthened the fort there in anticipation of a brutal winter. There was, however, no word from Tonti.

La Salle's spirits soon revived, and strong willed as ever, he set about making new plans for an expedition to the Mississippi and a renewed attempt to colonize the Illinois Valley. Now, he proposed a grand federation of the Algonquians against the Iroquois, with himself at the head. He obtained the acquiescence of a band of Abenaki and Mohicans, refugees from the the fury of the New England Puritans in King Philip's War; the agreement of the local Miami; the allegiance of the Shawnee; and tentative approval from the brutalized Illinois, who were slowly returning to the killing ground that had been their home. After making arrangements for a huge multitribal conference to be held at the St. Joseph in autumn, La Salle set off for Michilimackinac in quest of word from Tonti. There, he found the ironhanded adventurer himself. Tonti told a harrowing tale of capture by the Iroquois; escape owing to the intercession of an Iroquois chief who knew and admired La Salle; a perilous journey up the Illinois to Lake Michigan and ultimately Green Bay punctuated by canoe capsizings and Indian ambush; and, finally, sanctuary in a Potawatomi village. Despite this hardship and adventure, Tonti pronounced himself eager and ready to explore the Mississippi.

An Iroquois warrior; a late-17th-century engraving by J. Grasset St. Sauveur. Historian Bernard De Voto wrote: "No Indians of North America ever showed greater ferocity than the Iroquois; no tribe had more talent for military organization; few tribes fought better."

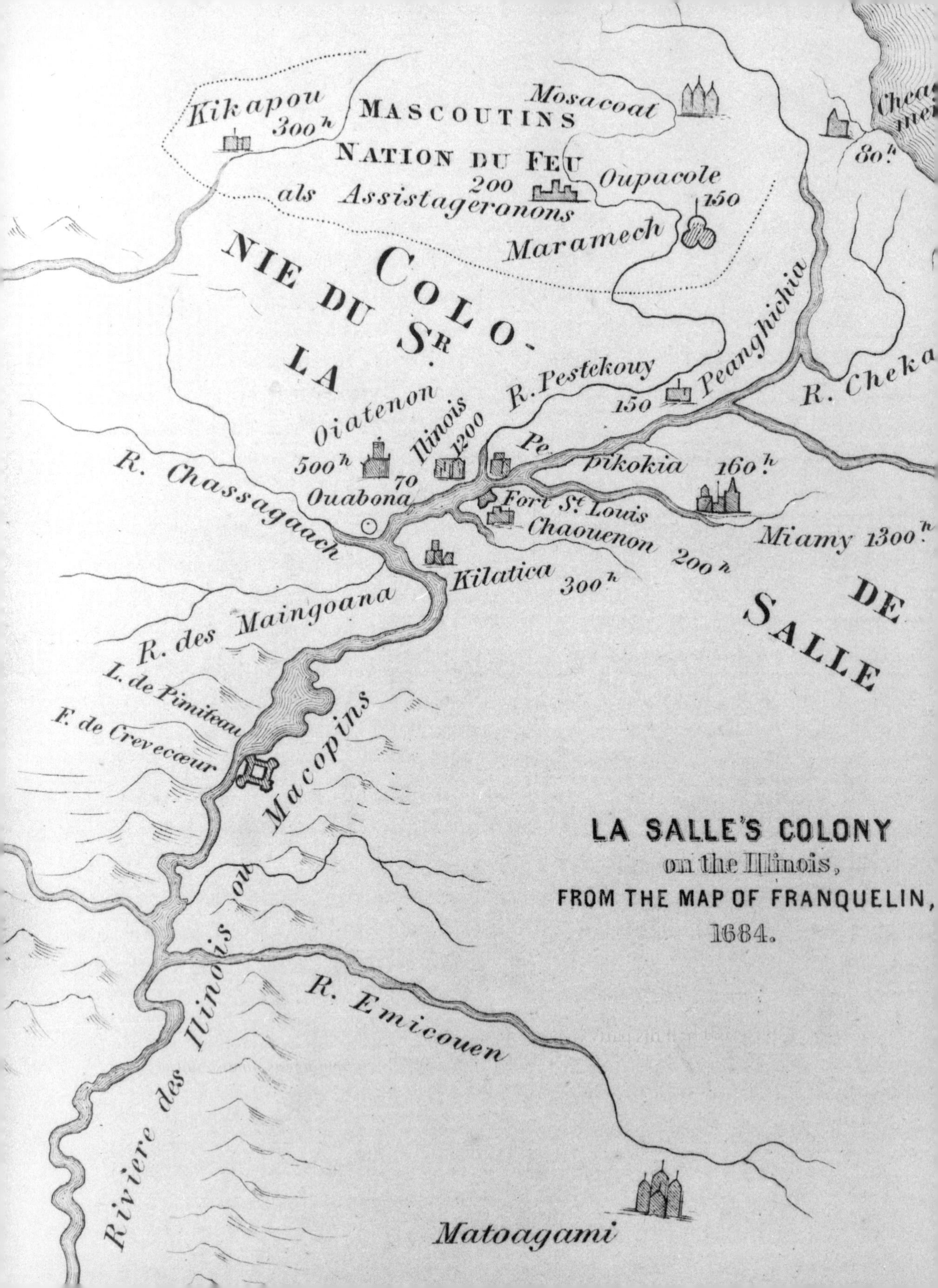

Kikapou 300 h

MASCOUTINS

Mosacoat

Cheag mer

80 h

NATION DU FEU

200

Oupacole

150

als Assistageronons

Maramech

LA

COLO-

NIE DU Sr.

R. Pestekouy

Peanghichia

R. Cheka

Oiatenon

Illinois 1200

150

R. Chassagaach

500 h

70

Pe

pikokia 160 h

Ouabona

Fort St Louis

Miamy 1300 h

Chaouenon 200 h

DE

R. des Maingoana

Kilatica 300 h

SALLE

L. de Pimiteau

F. de Creveceur

Macopins

LA SALLE'S COLONY
on the Illinois,
FROM THE MAP OF FRANQUELIN,
1684.

R. Emicouen

Riviere des Ilinois ou

Matoagami

On the Great River

After returning to Fort Frontenac for provisions, La Salle left the mouth of the St. Joseph in late December 1681. With him, in 12 to 15 small canoes, traveled 22 Frenchmen, 18 Indian hunters and guides, 10 Indian women, and 3 Indian children. Having learned from experience of the dangers of dividing his party, La Salle intended this time to keep his group together. After pausing for a spell at the mouth of the Illinois, on February 13, La Salle and his party entered the Mississippi.

By late February, La Salle and the others had arrived in the vicinity of present-day Memphis, Tennessee. Here a member of the expedition, gunsmith Pierre Prudhomme, got lost in the woods while hunting. When the search party reported seeing evidence of Indians in the area, La Salle ordered a small fort built, which he named after Prudhomme. Leaving Tonti and 16 men to guard the rude structure, La Salle and the others set out on a reconnaissance. In their absence, a member of Tonti's party, the voyageur Gabriel Barbier, captured two Chickasaw Indians.

After the Chickasaw had informed him that their village was located only a short distance away, La Salle set out with the captives and half his party to see if he could locate Prudhomme there. When the village proved to be much farther away than indicated, La Salle sent one of the Chickasaw ahead with friendly greetings and various gifts. He asked that a meeting be arranged with the village elders

A member of La Salle's expedition drew this 1684 map of his colony on the Illinois River. La Salle had earlier told correspondents in France that the Illinois country "is nearly all so beautiful and so fertile; so free from forests, and so full of meadows, brooks, and rivers; so abounding in fish, game, and venison."

at a spot farther down the river, but Prudhomme surfaced soon afterward and the appointment was never kept.

On or around March 12, the explorers reached their first Arkansas village. On drawing near to the settlement, which they could not make out because of a thick fog, they were alarmed by the sound of beating drums. After crossing over to the opposite side of the river, they erected a fortification in less than half an hour. Soon, the Arkansas, who had apparently been informed that the Frenchmen were traveling down the river, came out in their canoes to look for them. The fog lifted, and, wrote a member of the party, "an [Arkansas] canoe came within bow-shot of . . . [us]. They shot an arrow. Had the shot been returned, it would have been a signal that we meant war; but, seeing that we did not shoot, they went back to their village and reported us to be men of peace." The chief of the Arkansas then sent back a second canoe with six men. After entering the hastily built fort, this delegation offered La Salle a calumet and invited him and the others to their village, where the Frenchmen were received with great hospitality. It soon became apparent that the Arkansas hoped the Frenchmen would join with them in their struggles against various enemies. La Salle skirted the issue, but he did offer the Arkansas the protection of the king of France and pronounced the tribe subjects of Louis XIV. Although it is doubtful that either party understood the other very well, La Salle's improvised ceremony apparently satisfied all concerned.

The explorers briefly visited several other nearby villages, then resumed their voyage. Sometime around March 22 they arrived among the Taensa Indians, who lived on Lake St. Joseph, in modern-day Tensas Parish, Louisiana. As soon as the Frenchmen had established camp, about seven or eight miles away from the Taensa settlement, Tonti, with a small party, set off to visit the village. There they discovered a native standard of living higher than any they had previously known. "Never was

I so surprised," Tonti claimed, "as when I entered into the cabin of the chief." It was 40 feet square, with mud walls 12 feet high and 2 feet thick, and had a large dome-shaped roof. Tonti "saw the chief seated on a camp bed, surrounded by more than 60 old men clothed in large white cloaks. . . . There was a cane torch in the middle of the cabin, whose four walls were decorated with several green copper shields and a number of paintings." Tonti told the chief that he had come to make an alliance with the Taensa and that he and his men were short of food. The next day, after Tonti had rejoined La Salle, "many canoes arrived, filled with food." Tonti returned to the Indian village, where this time he was struck by the religious practices of the Taensa:

> The Taensas have a god; . . . we saw a temple opposite the chief's house in which there is a sort of altar and at the summit three eagles facing the rising sun. This temple is enclosed rather in the manner of a redoubt. On top of the thick walls surrounding it they place the heads of their enemies, whom they have killed in war—to guard it day and night.

After spending four nights with the Taensa, the explorers continued on their way. Thirty miles downstream they spotted a canoe crossing the river in front of them. "We gave chase," Tonti reports, "and my canoe, which was the fastest, drew ahead of all the others. As I came alongside the pirogue [a canoe made from a hollow tree trunk] I was greatly surprised to see the entire river-bank lined with savages who were armed with bows and arrows."

La Salle's leadership may be questioned in terms of his ability to claim the loyalty of his men, but he apparently possessed a particularly strong ability to form good relations with the Indians. His naturally grave manner, which was such an irritant to many of his companions, seems to have been appreciated by the Indians he encountered, who put a premium on dignity and solemnity of bearing. Unlike

A hand-drawn map of the upper Mississippi River valley, probably from the early 18th century. La Salle began his descent of the great river somewhat lower than the region shown here, at the confluence of the Mississippi and the Illinois, near present-day Grafton, Illinois.

This engraving of La Salle on the Mississippi was based on a sketch by Father Louis Hennepin, a Belgian cleric who accompanied the expedition. Hennepin was so fascinated by exploration that before joining La Salle he often lurked behind doorways in disreputable waterfront taverns in order to overhear sailors talking about their adventures.

so many of the European conqueror-explorers of the New World, he seems, except on one occasion, to have succeeded in avoiding violent encounters with the indigenous inhabitants of the regions he traveled through, who were, of course, the true discoverers of North America and its myriad wonders. This time, as on other occasions, La Salle kept his head, as Tonti relates:

> M. de La Salle shouted to me to come back, which I did. We went on and encamped opposite them. Afterwards, M. de La Salle expressing to me a wish to meet them peacefully, I offered to carry to them the calumet. I embarked, and crossed to the other side. . . . [T]hey joined their hands, as a sign they wished to be friends; I, who had but one hand, told our men to do the same thing.

The Indians with whom the Frenchmen now made peace were Natchez. At the invitation of their chiefs, La Salle and some of his men spent some nights at a settlement several miles inland. While at this village, La Salle heard of an important chief who was the representative of the main Natchez settlement, which was located some 20 miles downstream. He set off in search of Fatherland, as the village was known, but got only as far as a smaller collection of dwellings known as Koroa. Nicholas de La Salle, a member of the expedition unrelated to its commander, observed that Koroa was

> situated on the side of a mountain which slopes down to the bank of the river. . . . The lodges are dome-shaped, supported from ground to roof with great reeds. They are 15 feet high, windowless, but with a square door 4 feet in height in every lodge. At night there is in each a lighted torch, made of canes tied together. . . . The people . . . have coverlets resembling cotton hammocks. With these they cover themselves about the waist, fastening them with a cord which has two great tassels at the end. . . . They adorn their lodges with great round plates of shining copper, made like pot covers.

Tonti added that the inhabitants of Koroa "cultivate the ground as well as hunt, and . . . [also] fish."

On April 3, farther downstream, the explorers spotted a settlement on the left bank of the river. On crossing over to it, a horrible sight met their eyes. A member of the expedition known to history only as Minet recorded the scene in his journal:

> [W]e noticed something like many people; [but] when we had landed, we saw that the crowds were crows, eagles, and other beasts that seek out carrion. We knew by this that the village had been destroyed. On approaching, we saw only carcasses of men and women, ruined huts, and others full of dead bodies, a coating of blood on the ground, and all their canoes broken and cut up with axes.

La Salle's canoe voyage down the Mississippi was punctuated by a series of triumphal ceremonies in which he took possession of land for Louis XIV and France. Here, Catlin has portrayed La Salle pronouncing the Arkansaw Indians subjects of Louis XIV, whose sovereignty they were willing to acknowledge so long as the French protected them from the Iroquois.

Shortly after witnessing this scene of devastation, the explorers made another grotesque discovery, which Minet also described:

> The next day . . . we met a canoe with three savages in it. As soon as they noticed people, they fled . . . , and, not being able to pass through the reeds and canes with their canoe . . . , they landed and took to the woods. We went to the canoe. There we found some smoked caiman [an alligator-like reptile] and . . . [some unidentifiable] ribs, which we took. . . . As hunger was pressing us, having only a little corn daily, we pounced on this meat. When we had eaten . . . [the ribs], we knew that . . . [they] were human by the bones and the taste, which was better than the caiman.

Having survived their accidental brush with cannibalism, two days later, on April 6, La Salle and his party arrived at a fork where the river divided into three channels. After camping on the bank of the westernmost one, the next day La Salle went down that branch, while Tonti explored the middle channel and a third member of the party reconnoitered the eastern fork. Several miles downstream, all three explorers came to the sea. Here, at last, revealing itself for the first time to European eyes, was the mouth of the Mississippi. Although the river's mouth pointed east-southeast—not south, as anticipated—the travelers had no doubt that they had reached the Gulf of Mexico.

On April 8, they turned back and reascended the river in search of an elevated spot, drier than the marshland by the sea, on which to formally lay claim to the region for France. The next day, near modern-day Venice, Louisiana, the French chanted a prayer, fired off a volley of shots, and shouted, "Vive le Roi!" (Long live the king!), while La Salle raised a large cross and a smaller post that bore the coat of arms of the royal family. In a loud voice, he proclaimed:

> In the name of the most high, mighty, invincible, and victorious Prince, Louis the Great, . . . King of France

(continued on page 81)

Painter and Explorer

King Louis XIV of France studies a chart while contemplating the proposal of La Salle (right) to colonize the Illinois Valley.

The American artist George Catlin, who painted the pictures seen on the following pages, deserves a mention in the annals of exploration for more than his artwork. Between 1831 and 1837, Catlin, who was 35 when he set out, traveled thousands of miles by canoe and horse—from St. Louis northwest up the Missouri and Mississippi, and as far south and east as Texas and Florida—in order to fulfill his life's dream, the creation of a complete artistic record of the American Indians as they lived in their native country. He covered as many miles as did Lewis and Clark on their epic trek, in the process painting hundreds of pictures of the Indians as they lived "before their native dignity and beauty and independence" were destroyed. Along with Lewis and Clark's *Journals* and Francis Parkman's *The California and Oregon Trail*, the letters and notes he wrote during his travels, collected as *North American Indians*, constitute one of the absolute classics of American wilderness writing. Catlin preferred to paint from life, but his interest in the mutually dependent, often destructive relationship between Indian and white culture on the frontier made La Salle a natural subject for him.

To the dismay of the Indians and the delight of
La Salle and Father Hennepin (foreground, left
of center), the Griffin is successfully launched.

While the Iroquois keep a wary watch from shore and their canoes, a red-cloaked La Salle drives the first bolt for the Griffin, *the ship he hoped would enable him to dominate the Great Lakes fur trade.*

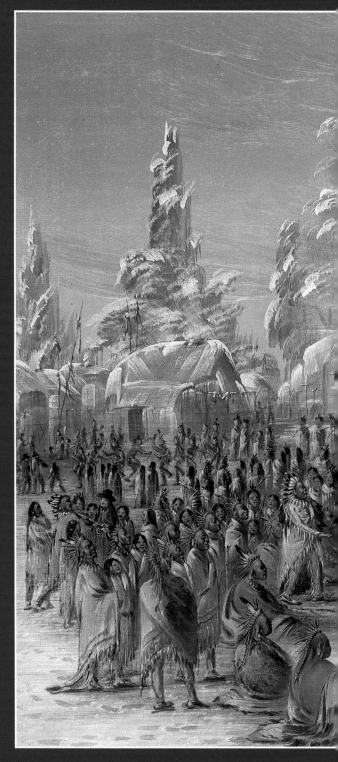

La Salle's Party Feasted in the Illinois Village, January 1680, *painted by Catlin in 1847–48. Catlin was entirely self-taught as an artist and is often criticized for his somewhat primitive technical skills, but his work is informed by a familiarity with the Indians and their way of life that was shared by very few of his contemporaries.*

Indians launch a canoe on the Nass River in British Columbia. The vessel is not one of the smaller, birchbark crafts that the Indians of the Great Lakes often used but a larger boat called by the French a pirogue, which was hewn out of a single tree trunk. Pirogues could be upwards of 50 feet long.

La Salle's party is greeted by the Ceni Indians of Texas in May 1686. The Cenis believed that newcomers were the returning souls of their departed kin. Catlin visited the Indians of Texas in the spring and summer of 1834.

An epic moment in the exploration of America:
La Salle's party enters the Mississippi River.

(continued from page 72)

and . . . Fourteenth of that name, . . . I . . . do now take
. . . possession of this country of Louisiana, the seas,
harbors, ports, bays, adjacent straits; and all the nations,
people, provinces, cities, towns, villages, mines, minerals,
fisheries, streams, and rivers, comprised in the extent of
said Louisiana, from the mouth of the great river St.
Louis, otherwise called the Ohio, . . . as also along the
. . . Mississippi, and the rivers which discharge themselves
therein, from its source beyond the country of the [Sioux]
. . . as far as its mouth at the sea, or Gulf of Mexico.

Although neither La Salle nor any of his contemporaries
had any idea of the true magnitude of the territory he had
laid such ambitious claim to, he did recognize that the
size and potential importance of the Mississippi Valley was
very great and that it was important to lay claim to it before
another European power did.

The ceremony completed, little else remained to be
done except return upriver. Hunger had become a serious
problem, and for several days the expedition subsisted on
potatoes and alligator meat. Neither proved to be a very

To the accompaniment of musket fire, hymns, and prayers, La Salle takes possession for France "of this country of Louisiana, the seas, harbors, ports, bays, adjacent straits, and all the nations, peoples, provinces, cities, towns, villages, mines, minerals, fisheries, streams and rivers, within the extent of the said Louisiana."

popular course. Above Tangipahoa, the burned-out village the party had seen earlier, La Salle managed to convince a group of Quinipissa to bring them some corn. The following night, while the travelers slept on shore, a Quinipissa war party attacked. A recent rain had soaked the weapons of the French, and in the confusion and darkness, with war whoops ringing through the soaked woods around them, they found it difficult to load and fire their muskets. Not that there was anything to aim at; although a hail of arrows descended on the French position, the Indians remained unseen, except for a trio of courageous (or foolish) warriors who attempted to sail their canoe right up on shore and into the French encampment and who were all dispatched, according to Minet, with a single shot. The battle lasted until sunrise, when the Indians fled, leaving behind them their tomahawks, bows, blankets, and canoes. Later that day, as the French departed, they were nearly ambushed a second time. To make sure that the Quinipissa did not return, the Frenchmen scalped two dead Indians and mounted their heads on posts, their faces turned in the direction of the Quinipissa villages.

A brief visit to Koroa confirmed that the region's inhabitants were no longer pleased about the continued presence of the intruders. After being feasted, the explorers found themselves surrounded by an estimated 1,600 braves, daubed in red and black, tomahawks at the ready. Only considerable blustering and brandishing of weapons—a few rounds were fired off into the air for show—enabled La Salle's party to reach the comparative safety of the river. Farther upriver, the Indians were more welcoming. The Taensa, especially, continued to be friendly, particularly once they learned of the ill treatment the French had given the Quinipissa.

Local animosity strengthened La Salle's resolution to reach the Illinois Valley quickly and attend to the large supply of furs he had stored at Fort Miami on the St. Joseph, but illness intervened. The disease, probably malaria or yellow fever contracted in the fetid swamps of the lower Mississippi, kept him supine for 40 days at Fort Prudhomme, which he entered borne on a litter by his men. Tonti and the majority of the expedition were sent on ahead to Fort Miami, where they retrieved the furs, and then on to Michilimackinac.

A partially restored La Salle reached Fort Crèvecœur on July 12 and then hurried on toward Michilimackinac, where bad news awaited him. La Salle had planned on gathering his furs and proceeding on to Quebec and then France in order to repay his creditors and report his discoveries, but he learned that it was not an opportune time to show himself at either location. The Iroquois were on the warpath again, and many blamed La Salle. The Iroquois were used to obtaining furs from the Illinois tribes and then trading them to the French, at a lucrative markup, but La Salle's colonization scheme threatened to draw the Illinois and other tribes into his orbit and eliminate the Iroquois role as brokers. The warfare was the Iroquois way of showing their displeasure with this turn of events, and it was threatening the flow of furs to New France. At Quebec, Intendant Duchesneau blamed La Salle:

> The improper conduct of Sieur de la Salle . . . has contributed considerably to cause [the Iroquois] to adopt this proceeding; for after he had obtained permission to discover the great river of Mississippi, and had, as he alleged, the grant of the Illinois, he no longer observed any terms with the Iroquois at Fort Frontenac. He ill-treated them, and avowed that he would convey arms and ammunition to the Illinois, and would die assisting them.

Charges like those leveled by Duchesneau gained greater currency than they might otherwise have because La Salle's ally and protector, Frontenac, had been recalled to France. The new governor, Joseph Antoine Le Febvre de La Barre, was not well-disposed toward La Salle, whom

La Salle's ambitious proclamation gave France nominal control over a massive wilderness empire of incomparable natural richness, but unlike England, France was never to succeed in populating its New World settlements sufficiently enough to hold them.

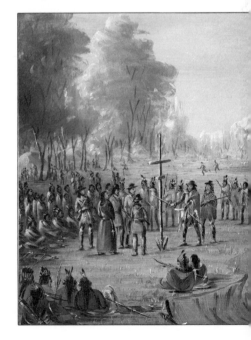

he regarded as a potential rival for power. It was La Barre's opinion, as expressed in a letter to the Marquis de Seignelay, Louis's new minister of the marine and colonies, that La Salle was trying to "build up an imaginary kingdom for himself." La Barre had handed over control of Fort Frontenac to the Sieur de la Chesnaye, claiming that La Salle had abandoned it and that it had to be kept in operation to counteract British influence on the Iroquois. In addition, the governor had made known his intentions of putting to an end all French trading activities in the Illinois Valley.

Recognizing that the best immediate action would be to avoid official circles, La Salle decided to return to the Illinois Valley immediately. Technically, there were still eight months remaining in the life of the royal license granting him special trading privileges. On the brink of financial ruin, he could not afford to lose this opportunity to redeem himself with his creditors. If he could spend the next eight months trading with the Indians of the interior, he might be able to accumulate enough furs to pay off some of his most pressing debts.

After writing to La Barre to formally announce his discoveries, La Salle left Michilimackinac and set off to join Tonti at Fort Crèvecœur. After his arrival there on December 30, La Salle immediately began constructing a second fort. This stronghold, which he named Fort St. Louis, was built atop Starved Rock, the 125-foot-high natural citadel overlooking the Illinois River. To symbolize the legitimacy and permanence of French settlement in the valley, La Salle ordered his men to plow the land around the fort and plant it with corn.

Once their fortress was secure, La Salle and Tonti began trading actively with various local tribes. The cache of furs at Fort St. Louis began to grow large, and as it did La Salle's future started to look brighter. Knowing that his presence in the valley would be hard to justify after his license expired, in April 1683, La Salle wrote La Barre

the first of three letters asking for an extension of his privileges. He received no response, but when the couriers that he sent east with furs began failing to return (some deserted, but the majority were detained by La Barre's officials), La Salle recognized that his situation was again desperate. In August he left Fort St. Louis under Tonti's command and set off for Quebec. Thirty-five miles up the Illinois he encountered a party of 30 canoes led by the Chevalier de Baugy, who had been sent by La Barre to assume command of Fort St. Louis. La Salle was ordered to Quebec.

Contemplating this calamitous turn of events, the unlucky explorer could see only one way to save himself. He decided that he must travel to Paris and somehow convince the king himself to save him from utter financial ruin.

A tragic flaw prevented La Salle from achieving all that he envisioned. Wrote Francis Parkman: "[La Salle] lacked that sympathetic power, the inestimable gift of the true leader of men, in which lies the difference between a willing and a constrained obedience. This solitary being, hiding his shyness under a cold reserve, could rouse no enthusiasm in his followers."

The Last
Expedition

By the time La Salle arrived in France in late December 1683 his plans had grown more ambitious. He now hoped to escape the interference of officials in Quebec by creating an independent colony on the mouth of the Mississippi, which, he planned to argue, would best be approached not from the interior but by sea. In Paris, he easily convinced Louis to reinstate his ownership of Fort Frontenac, but it proved more difficult to win the king's support for his new colonization scheme.

With a pair of ambitious lobbyists, Eusèbe Renaudot and the Abbé Claude Bernou, La Salle soon became involved in a bizarre scheme to pique Louis's interest by proposing that his colony be used as a base from which to attack New Spain. In order to make his proposal more attractive, La Salle presented the king with a map that greatly distorted the true path of the Mississippi by making it appear as if the river veered west, leaving its mouth on the western coast of the Gulf of Mexico, in present-day Texas—an ideal location from which to harass the Spanish and raid their silver mines. Through this distortion, La Salle created confusion about the actual location of the Mississippi's mouth, which remained a mystery until 12 years after his death. He further led the king to believe that the French would be aided in their efforts against the Spanish by the powerful Algonquian confederacy he had attempted to build in the Illinois Valley years before,

La Salle's ships unload at Matagorda Bay where, either by mistake or intent to deceive, his expedition to find the mouth of the Mississippi landed.

which now, he told the credulous Louis and his ministers, numbered 15,000 strong.

By March 1684 the king had fallen for the bait. Louis granted La Salle control of all the forts he had already constructed, command over all the men he would need for his enterprise, and permission to establish a new French colony. Instead of the single vessel he had requested, La Salle received two: the 36-gun *Joly* and the much smaller *Belle*, the first of which was to return to France after escorting the colonists to their new home. With money he now found easy to raise, La Salle chartered two more ships, a large cargo vessel called the *Aimable* and a small ketch known as the *St. François*. Although the details of the expedition were a closely guarded secret, La Salle quickly gathered a large number of volunteers, among them his brother Abbé Jean Cavelier, his nephew Crevel de Moranget, the Recollet priests Fathers Zénobe Membré, Anastus Douay, and Maxime Le Clerc, and Henri Joutel, a soldier who wrote the principal account of the expedition.

Although there were a number of very able men among the roughly 300 passengers, whose number included women and children for the founding of a permanent settlement, many of those conscripted to serve as soldiers or craftsmen left something to be desired. As Father Le Clerc observed:

> Those who were appointed [to do the recruiting], while M. de la Salle was at Paris, picked up 150 soldiers, mere wretched beggars soliciting alms, many too deformed and unable to form a musket. The sieur de la Salle had also given orders at Rochelle to engage three or four mechanics in each trade; the selection was, however, so bad, that when they came to the destination, and were set to work, it was seen that they knew nothing at all.

La Salle's fleet of four ships left La Rochelle on July 24, 1684. From the beginning tension ran high between La

Salle and the captain of the *Joly*, Sieur de Beaujeu. Beaujeu was annoyed by La Salle's high-handedness, his paranoid secretiveness about the object of their voyage, and his lack of knowledge about naval affairs; La Salle resented the king's directive that gave Beaujeu, who was a captain in the royal navy, full authority over the fleet while it was at sea. He also suspected Beaujeu's loyalty, mainly because his wife was well known for her devotion to the Jesuits, whom La Salle, as ever, suspected of scheming to undermine his mission. He feared as well that Beaujeu planned to actually attack certain Spanish settlements, whereas La Salle had simply floated that possibility as a means of persuading Louis to grant him what he wished, knowing all the while that the area he meant to colonize was far from Spanish territory.

The captain was among those at the French court who believed that the explorer was no longer in his right mind. Years of pushing himself to the limit of his capabilities, constant anxiety about the state of his affairs, and especially his illness had undermined La Salle's mental equilibrium. He suffered from frequent high fevers and delirium, his latent suspicion of others had now blossomed into full-blown paranoia (Tonti, back in America, was now one of those La Salle mumbled darkly about having betrayed him), and secretiveness had become an obsession. In a letter, Beaujeu responded to a friend's inquiry as to his impressions of La Salle:

> You ask how I get along with M. de la Salle. Don't you know that this man is impenetrable, and that there is no knowing what he thinks of one? . . . His distrust is incredible. If he sees one of his people speak to the rest, he suspects something, and is gruff with them. . . . There are very few people who do not think that his brain is touched. I have spoken to some who have known him 20 years. They all say that he was always rather visionary.

After a painfully slow two-month voyage the expedition

The Marquis de Seignelay, Louis's minister of the marine and colonies, was the son of Jean-Baptiste Colbert. Seignelay wanted to transform La Salle's colonization scheme into a plan for an attack on Spain's possessions, particularly its silver mines, in New Mexico.

reached Santo Domingo (as the island of Hispaniola, now home to the countries of Haiti and the Dominican Republic, was sometimes known), where its problems multiplied. On approaching the island, the *St. François*, with its irreplaceable cargo of provisions and tools, was captured by Spanish privateers. La Salle, already ill, became desperately sick on hearing of the ship's loss. While he lay prostrate in a rented garret ashore, sweating, trembling, and hallucinating, some of the soldiers and sailors deserted, and others indulged in wild revelry that left them dissipated and disease ridden.

By the end of November, La Salle was well enough for the voyage to be resumed. The expedition passed through the Yucatán Channel and entered the Gulf of Mexico, a forbidden zone the Spanish had declared off-limits to all but their own vessels. On December 28, land was spotted. The fleet drew nearer the shore and began hugging the coast in search of an outlet large enough to be the Mississippi.

For reasons that historians and biographers still hotly dispute, the four ships somehow bypassed the Mississippi and wound up more than 400 miles to the west, at Matagorda Bay in present-day Texas. Some believe that La Salle intentionally misguided the small fleet's pilots and navigators in order to situate himself closer to New Spain. Others argue that he simply made an honest mistake, that because in 1682 he had been unable to record the longitude of the mouth of the river, he did not know where to look for it on his return voyage. Yet another explanation is that he sailed past the Mississippi in an attempt to lose Beaujeu and the *Joly*, whom he had ordered to return to France, and was returning to the river when the disobedient captain came upon him at Matagorda Bay, at which point La Salle felt he had no choice but to pretend that this was the mouth of the Mississippi, as he had presented it on the doctored map he had drawn for Louis. The Abbé Cavelier claimed that after the inadvertent separation in

By the time La Salle arrived in Paris in late 1683 to petition Louis for permission to colonize Louisiana, illness and travail had played havoc with his reason. His natural mistrust of others had become a crippling paranoia, and he found it difficult to make decisions.

the Gulf of the *Joly*, which carried most of the soldiers and colonists, and the two other remaining vessels, which were laden primarily with supplies, La Salle sailed too far west in search for the missing Beaujeu and never regained his bearings.

On February 20, 1685, La Salle put his colonists ashore at Matagorda Bay. The newcomers were greeted by "an Indian nation of four hundred to five hundred members, dressed in skins of a kind of wild ox," according to Beaujeu, "who had never seen Europeans, nor were they familiar with tobacco." At first the Indians were friendly, but there was a "falling-out over some trivial thing, which cost the lives of three Frenchmen, whom [they] killed with arrows."

During this encounter a further disaster was developing. On following the other ships into Matagorda Bay the *Aimable* ran aground and was wrecked. A sudden storm prevented the French from salvaging more than a fraction of the ship's cargo, and for a second time irreplaceable supplies were lost. Joutel wrote that La Salle and most of the members of the expedition believed that the shipwreck had been an intentional act on the part of another disloyal captain, Sieur d'Aigron.

The colonists, huddled together on a narrow sandbar without fresh water and with little food, quickly fell prey to dysentery and other diseases. Five or six died each day; the remainder subsisted on the occasional oyster and marsh grass, which they boiled in the brackish water of the bay. Beaujeu, with whom La Salle had largely repaired his relationship, was in a hurry to return to France with the king's ship, but he offered to first sail to Martinique to obtain fresh supplies. La Salle rejected this suggestion, probably out of a desire to keep his presence at the bay secret. The *Joly* set sail on March 12, but in France that summer Beaujeu was unable to convince the court to send help for the colonists, as the expedition had already proved unusually expensive. Seignelay did have the mutinous (or merely incompetent) d'Aigron thrown into the prison tower at La Rochelle, but that did La Salle and his charges little good.

As soon as Beaujeu was gone, the colonists constructed a primitive fortress from driftwood, uprooted trees, and the spars and timbers of the wrecked *Aimable*, which they armed with cannons Beaujeu had hauled off the *Joly*. While La Salle set off with 50 men in 5 canoes to explore a river at the head of the bay, the colonists, in historian Francis Parkman's words, huddled "among tents and hovels, bales, boxes, casks, spars, dismounted cannon, and pens for fowl and swine." At night, Indians—not the friendly Algonquians La Salle had promised—crept around the fort's exterior, howling like wolves and terrifying its occupants. By day, the Indians set the nearby prairie ablaze, hoping thereby to drive off the unwelcome newcomers. The colonists continued to sicken and die. This handful of "dejected men and homesick women," Parkman wrote, had been charged to "hold for France a region large as half of Europe."

Things did not improve when La Salle decided to relocate the colony. Historians have traditionally placed the site of the new settlement on La Vache (now known as the Lavaca), as La Salle named the river he had found, but archaeological evidence suggests that it may actually have been on the west bank of nearby Garcitas Creek, some five miles from its mouth. Most of the colonists were moved there in early summer, but when Joutel, who had been left in command at the entrance to Matagorda Bay, arrived somewhat later on he was "amaz'd to see Things so ill begun and so little advanc'd. . . . [T]he Seed and Grain put into the Ground, was either lost through Drought, or eaten by Birds or Beasts. There were several Dead, . . . [and] many sick." Furthermore, there was "no Shelter but a little square Place stak'd in."

Despite the crying need for shelter, La Salle's decision to erect a large wooden house—to be used by all—in the center of the settlement only increased the resentment and despair of the colonists. With no horses or carts available, the men and women were forced to drag felled trees to the camp over irregular ground and through heavy underbrush. "This excessive Toil," Joutel recalled, together with "the poor Sustenance the labouring Men had, . . . [and] the Uneasiness Monsieur de la Sale was under . . . , which often made him insult the Men, . . . afflicted very many so sensibly, that they visibly declin'd, and above thirty dy'd." After this first backbreaking project was completed, La Salle supervised the building of a fort, which he named St. Louis. Despite this flurry of activity, his mind was again beset by the gloom into which he now frequently descended, and the mood of the colony reflected his morbid temperament. Misfortune continued; each day the cries of the sick and dying could be heard, and the colony's master carpenter, clearly one of its most

La Salle's men row ashore at Matagorda Bay, a swampy, pestilential site where the would-be colonists suffered greatly. Despite the various disasters that befell the expedition, La Salle's "intrepidity did not forsake him, and he applied himself, without grieving, to remedy what might be," according to Henri Joutel, a member of his party.

valuable citizens, simply vanished while out hunting. The anxiety at the settlement increased with the discovery by La Salle and some of his men of a village, in Abbé Cavelier's words, "enclosed with a kind of wall made of clay and sand, and fortified with little towers at intervals." Inside this abandoned settlement was found a copper plate with the arms of Spain engraved on it and various other objects that clearly indicated that Spaniards had once lived there. The find might have pleased the departed Beaujeu, but for the struggling colony the Spanish were now to be feared as much as the Indians.

La Salle had long since been forced to admit that neither Matagorda Bay nor La Vache led to the Mississippi. Therefore, on October 31, 1685, he set out with 50 men in search of the great river, leaving Joutel in charge at St. Louis, which fared well under his supervision. New lodgings and a chapel were built, and the colonists' diet improved with the discovery that the nearby prairies were rich in deer, buffalo, rabbit, turkeys, snipe, grouse, and plover. Buffalo were especially plentiful—Joutel reported seeing herds of 6,000 beasts thundering across the prairie, but bringing one down proved quite an adventure. Unaware that a buffalo rarely falls at once unless hit near the spine, Joutel watched in amazement as the powerful shaggy creatures seemingly shrugged off shots at point-blank range and lumbered away. Once, Father Douay attempted to head off a buffalo that was jogging away after Joutel had shot it. The priest made the mistake of jumping in front of the wounded animal, which nonchalantly butted the cleric with its head and sent him flying. On another occasion, Father Membré, much to the amusement of Joutel, made the mistake of tapping a fallen and presumably dead buffalo on the snout with the butt of his gun. The enraged ruminant quickly roused itself and trampled the rash clergyman. Joutel also derived some hilarity from the sight of Father Le Clerc, his escape hampered by his long hassock, in which his legs kept on getting entangled, scurrying across the prairie with a large wild boar in hard pursuit. The motive of the animal perplexed Joutel, who confessed, "I do not know what spite the beast had against him, whether for a beating or some other offense." On other days, Joutel amused himself by shooting alligators and rattlesnakes. The latter varmints were especially troublesome, as they had a habit of biting the colony's pigs and goats. Joutel claimed to be able to restore the animals to health by the use of a special salve he had brought from France.

Joutel's mirthfulness extended to his governance of the colony. Although he always remained loyal to La Salle, he was not blind to his shortcomings, and whereas La Salle's depressions and profound mournfulness had a tendency to overawe the colonists, Joutel sought always to sow good cheer. He described his efforts to ease the worry of the colonists about their plight:

> We did what we could to amuse ourselves and drive away care. I encouraged our people to dance and sing in the evenings; for, when M. de la Salle was among us, pleasure was often banished. Now there is no use in being melancholy on such occasions. It is true that M. de la Salle had no great cause for merrymaking, after all his losses and disappointment; but his troubles made others suffer as well.

The disheartened members of La Salle's expedition make camp under towering cypress trees near Matagorda Bay.

Meanwhile, La Salle's band headed east from Matagorda Bay, with the *Belle*, the expedition's last remaining vessel, coasting alongside of them. After deciding that it was unnecessary for the *Belle* to follow them any longer, La Salle ordered the ship's pilot to go with five men to make soundings for a suitable anchorage. Several nights later, while camped on a beach, the pilot and his men were killed by Indians. When they did not return, La Salle sent a search party, which found their remains "scattered about . . . and almost devoured by Wolves or Wild Dogs."

Following this disaster, La Salle ordered the captain of

(continued on page 98)

Tapping the Source

For more than a century after La Salle's death, there remained one great unsolved mystery about the Mississippi: Where did it originate? It was generally accepted that the river began among the network of lakes and rivers that cover northern Minnesota, but there was much dispute over which body of water was the actual source. In 1805, President Thomas Jefferson, who had a tremendous interest in the geography of the West, commissioned a lieutenant in the U.S. Army, Zebulon Pike, to discover the Mississippi's source. Pike's reconnaissance convinced him that Leech Lake, in present-day Cass County, was the birthplace of the Father of Waters, but few people accepted his hypothesis. The mystery remained.

In 1820, Lewis Cass, governor of the Michigan Territory, which included present-day Michigan, Wisconsin, and a sizable portion of Minnesota, mounted an expedition to the upper Mississippi. The purpose of this mission was to search for mineral deposits and to chart the northern part of the territory with an eye toward future settlement. Serving as mineralogist to this party of exploration was a 27-year-old New Yorker, Henry Rowe Schoolcraft, whose study *A View of the Lead Mines of Missouri* had greatly impressed the secretary of war, John C. Calhoun.

Schoolcraft was born in upstate Hamilton, New York, on March 28, 1793. He was trained in the nuances of glassmaking by his father, who had also enjoyed a successful military career. As a young man, Schoolcraft supervised glassworks in western New York, Vermont, and New Hampshire, but he found himself, like many Americans of the era, drawn toward the western frontier. He believed that "information, of such a wide and varied region, whose boundaries were but ill-defined, must be interesting at such a period," he wrote later. "With such views I resolved to go west."

His foray down the Ohio River and into Arkansas and Missouri led to the account that brought him to Calhoun's notice. On May 24, 1820, therefore, as 1 of a party of 34 men that included voyageurs, Indian guides, and a military escort, Schoolcraft set out from Detroit. Traveling in long birch-bark canoes, the party made its way to the western end of Lake Superior, up the St. Louis River, and down the Sandy Lake River to the Mississippi. Over several weeks' time it followed the Mississippi to Upper Red Cedar Lake, which Cass pronounced to be the river's source and renamed after himself.

Although Schoolcraft penned the official account of the expedition, he did not agree with its conclusions about the Mississippi's origin. For 12 years, other responsibilities—during this time, he served as Indian agent at Sault Ste. Marie, founded the Michigan Historical Society, and got married—prevented him from testing his theories, but in 1832 he led a 35-man expedition in quest of the source. Schoolcraft and his party initially followed the same route as the Cass expedition, but with the guidance of a Chippewa Indian named Oza

Windib, they eventually made their way westward and then southward beyond Cass Lake. On July 13, 1832, Schoolcraft and his men reached the Mississippi's source, "a beautiful sheet of water, seven or eight miles in extent, lying among hills. . . . The waters are transparent and bright, and reflect a foliage produced by the elm, lynn, maple and cherry." Schoolcraft dubbed this pleasant body of water Lake Itasca, from his rather ungrammatical understanding of a Latin phrase meaning true source. There, on the lake's single island, in a modest counterpart to La Salle's ceremony at the river's mouth 150 years earlier, Schoolcraft raised an American flag on the trunk of a felled spruce tree.

Henry Rowe Schoolcraft

(continued from page 95)

the ship, Teissier, to pull out into the bay, drop anchor, and remain in place until receiving further orders. After hiding their canoes, La Salle and his party continued eastward for some distance, in the process encountering several Indian tribes, some of them hostile. In the territory of a friendly tribe, whose identity has remained unclear, they discovered the mouth of a large river—most likely the Trinity, which flows into Galveston Bay, or even the Sabine, which constitutes the southern border of the modern states of Texas and Louisiana.

Seeing that the surrounding country was rich in natural resources and that the local Indians appeared to be friendly, La Salle decided to reestablish his colony along the banks of this river. Accordingly, he and the others headed back toward the settlement at Matagorda Bay, from which La Salle planned to transport the colonists by means of the *Belle*. When they reached the spot where they had left the *Belle*, however, the ship was no longer there. Ordering the Sieurs Barbier and Bihorel, along with a few others, to search for the vessel, La Salle continued on his trek and arrived back at the colony with the remainder of his party in the middle of March 1686. After an absence of more than four months La Salle and his men were, in the words of Joutel, "in bad Condition, their Clothes ragged . . . ; most of them had not Hats, and their Linen was no better; however the Sight of Monsieur de la Sale rejoy'd us all."

The elation of the colonists was short-lived. Soon after La Salle's arrival, Barbier, Bihorel, and the others returned with the disturbing news that they could find no trace of the *Belle*. La Salle immediately suspected that the captain and his crew had deserted; several months later, however, it was discovered that the *Belle* had been wrecked and nearly its entire crew drowned. Aboard it were crucial provisions and all of La Salle's records and personal papers, but even more important was that the small ship had represented the colony's only practical means of resupplying

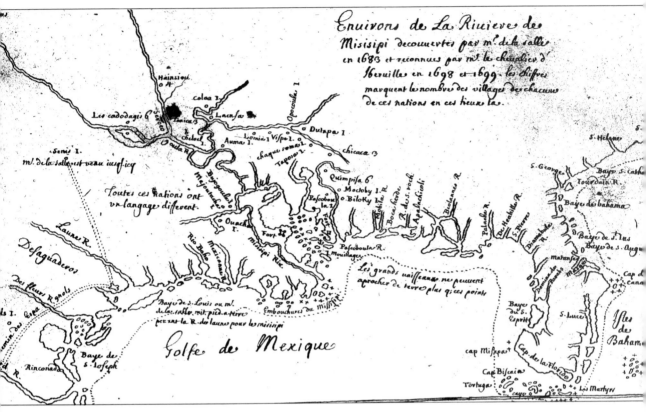

La Salle's deception in presenting his plan to Louis meant that for many years afterward great confusion existed about the exact location of the mouth of the Mississippi. Finally, in 1699, the Frenchman Pierre Le Moyne, Sieur d'Iberville, explored the Gulf of Mexico and cleared up the mystery. This is Iberville's hand-drawn map of the region.

itself and notifying the rest of the world of its whereabouts.

News of the disappearance of the *Belle* brought on a recurrence of La Salle's sickness. Once again, he fell dangerously ill, and for several days he lingered near death, but his remarkable constitution rose to the challenge. During his convalescence, a plan formed in his mind. If he traveled far enough in a northeasterly direction, he reasoned, he must inevitably come to the Mississippi. Once he had reached the river he could make his way up to the Illinois country and then on to Quebec, where he would secure aid for the colonists.

On April 22, 1686, having once more placed Joutel in charge of the colony, La Salle set out to realize this plan. With him went 20 men, including his brother and Father Douay. Traveling by land, tramping mile after endless mile, they made only slow progress. Prairies alternated with woodland, and the area's profusion of rivers posed a constant challenge. Father Douay described their improvised method for traversing these streams:

> One of our men, with an axe on his back, swam over to the other side, a second followed at once; they then cut down the largest trees, while others on our side did the same. These trees were cut so as to fall on each side into the river, where meeting, they formed a kind of bridge on which we easily passed. This invention we had recourse to more than thirty times in our journeys.

After crossing the Brazos, the Trinity, and many other smaller watercourses, La Salle and his party came upon a group of villages inhabited by Ceni Indians. When the Indians first caught sight of the white men, according to Douay, they wept "bitterly for a good quarter of an hour. It is their custom when they see any who come from afar, because it reminds them of their dead relatives whom they suppose on a long journey, from which they await their return." Thereafter, the Cenis treated the Frenchmen "with all possible friendship."

After spending several days among the Cenis, La Salle and the others pressed onward. Some time later they came to another group of villages, where they found many objects of Spanish design. The inhabitants of these villages were friendly, and the Frenchmen acquired horses and food from them. With lifted spirits, La Salle and the others continued eastward. Soon, however, both La Salle and his nephew Crevel de Moranget were stricken with fever. For two months the party was forced to camp near the Sabine River while waiting for the men to regain their strength. Upon recovery, La Salle determined to return to St. Louis. The ammunition was nearly spent, a few of the men had died of exhaustion and disease, another had been devoured by an alligator, some had deserted, and most of the rest were sick, tired, and hungry.

La Salle arrived at St. Louis sometime in August. Only 8 of the 20 men who had gone with him made it back; all told, just 40 colonists remained at New France's Texas outpost. Initial jubilation at La Salle's return soon gave way to a pervasive gloom as the colonists realized the implications of the failure of their leader's mission. The Abbé Cavelier observed:

> We had imagined that the king would send us two or three ships. But after having waited for years, we did not know what to think. Sometimes we thought that a ship might well have entered the Mississippi without our knowing it, and other times we imagined that the king believing us lost had forgotten all about us.

Recognizing the seriousness of the situation, La Salle began planning a second attempt to reach the Illinois Valley

Although La Salle has been criticized for many things, few ever doubted his courage. In January 1687, he left Fort St. Louis in an attempt to reach the Mississippi and eventually Montreal to obtain rescue for his desperate colony.

La Salle's assassin fires from the cover of some undergrowth. The murderers scared off Father Douay, preventing him from performing the final sacraments over his slain comrade, then stripped La Salle naked, spit on him and mocked him, and left his corpse for the wolves.

almost immediately upon his return to St. Louis, but in the early fall he fell deathly ill once more. It was not until January 1687 that he felt up to undertaking such a strenuous journey. This time he took a party of 16, including his nephew de Moranget, Joutel, and Douay. Gabriel Barbier was left in charge of the colony during La Salle's absence. Before setting off on the seventh day of the New Year, the members of the expedition said their farewells to those remaining behind. "We took our Leaves," Joutel wrote, "with so much Tenderness and Sorrow, as if we had all presaged, that we should never see each other more."

La Salle led his band along the same route as on their previous attempt. The men hunted for food, improvised shelters when necessary, and fashioned shoes out of buffalo hide when their own wore out. Nearly every day they met Indians, most of whom were friendly. By the beginning of March they had arrived in the country of the Cenis, where once again they were well received.

Around March 15, after crossing the Trinity River, they established camp at a site near present-day Navasota, Texas. Provisions were running low; La Salle recalled that on his last journey he had stored some food at a spot several miles away, and he ordered several of the men to retrieve it. On the way back to camp, this party killed two buffalo and sent a man named Saget ahead to ask La Salle for horses to transport the meat. The others remained behind to dress the carcasses.

On being apprised of the situation, La Salle ordered de Moranget, Saget, and a colonist named de Marle to bring in the meat, but a quarrel ensued after de Moranget, who possessed a touch of his uncle's hard-driving style, found fault with the way the hunters had prepared the carcasses and accused them of setting aside the best meat for themselves. Two of the men, Liotot and Duhaut, already had reason to hate de Moranget, who on his uncle's orders had punished them after they defied La Salle's edict against sleeping with Indian women. Duhaut had also earned La Salle's wrath by deserting on an earlier expedition. Enlisting several other men to help them, they resolved to murder de Moranget and set upon him that night with an ax as he lay sleeping. Several blows to the head did the job. Saget and a Shawnee Indian hunter named Nica, who were both extremely loyal to La Salle, then received similar treatment.

Having committed themselves to murder and mutiny, the conspirators realized that they would not be safe until they killed La Salle himself. Presently, La Salle became anxious over the absence of his men, and on the morning of March 19, 1687, he resolved to set out, together with Father Douay, in search of the missing party. He must have felt some premonition of disaster, for as he traveled, wrote Douay, La Salle spoke of "nothing but matters of piety, grace, and predestination; enlarging on the debt he owed to God, who had saved him from so many perils during more than 20 years of travel in America. . . . Suddenly, I saw him overwhelmed with a profound sense of sadness, for which he himself could not account."

As La Salle drew near to where the murderers waited, he spotted two eagles flying overhead. Thinking that the hunters might be nearby and that the birds had been attracted by the dead buffalo, he let off a shot. This sound alerted the conspirators to La Salle's presence, and they quickly laid a trap for him. Duhaut and Liotot ran to a spot near where La Salle stood and hid in a clump of brush with their guns cocked. Meanwhile, another plotter, 17-year-old L'Archevêque, advanced out into the open and headed directly toward La Salle. When La Salle caught sight of this solitary figure he demanded to know where de Moranget was. L'Archevêque answered him vaguely, then began hurling a stream of insults, all the while edging backward toward the spot where Duhaut and Liotot lay hidden. Suddenly, as La Salle drew near, Duhaut fired a single, well-aimed shot. La Salle fell down dead on the

This page comes from a manuscript written by Abbé Jean Cavelier, La Salle's brother, describing the tragic final expedition. Abbé Jean escaped the ill-fated colony and reached safety at a trading post established by Tonti on the Arkansas River, but he kept his brother's death a secret until he arrived in France many months later.

spot. As the terrified Douay watched, the murderers stripped naked La Salle's corpse and left it in the grass for the wolves and the scavengers.

So ended the life of René-Robert Cavelier, Sieur de La Salle, the tormented explorer of the Mississippi. Of those who knew him, Joutel left perhaps the best appraisal of his divided, contradictory character:

> He had a Capacity and Talent to make his Enterprise successful; his Constancy and Courage and his extraordinary Knowledge in Arts and Sciences, which rendered him fit for any Thing, together with an indefatigable Body, which made him surmount all Difficulties, would have procur'd a glorious Issue to his Undertaking, had not all those excellent Qualities been counterbalanced by too haughty a Behaviour, which sometimes made him insupportable, and by a Rigidness towards those that were under his Command, which at last drew on him an implacable Hatred, and was the Occasion of his Death.

Following La Salle's death most of the remaining colonists were either killed by Indians or captured by the Spanish. The conspirators turned on one another and committed several more murders; Joutel, Douay, and the Abbé Cavelier made it to safety at a trading post the tireless Tonti had established on the Arkansas River. Like so many of the great explorers, La Salle benefited little, if at all, from his work, but his historical legacy is undeniable. Although from the strictly geographic point of view La Salle's discoveries were not particularly impressive—he merely finished off what Jolliet and Marquette had virtually completed before him—he remains a figure of singular importance in the history of the Mississippi Valley. He established good relations with numerous Indian tribes, built a chain of forts across much of the continent, and claimed for France enormous stretches of territory. La Salle failed in his colonization attempts, but it was his efforts that provided much of the impetus for the eventual creation of Louisiana, as the vast French territory west of the Mississippi came to be known. Louisiana encompassed the better part of 14 present-day states and stretched from the Gulf of Mexico almost to Canada and from the Mississippi as far west as Idaho, an expanse almost as vast as that which La Salle took possession of for his monarch in April 1682.

La Salle's life seems, in retrospect, to have been an especially hard one, cruel even—devoid of creature comforts; rife with hardship, denial, and betrayal; unredeemed by riches, glory (at least during his own span of years), or even love. La Salle was, in Parkman's words,

> serious in all things, incapable of the lighter pleasures, incapable of repose, finding no joy but in the pursuit of great designs, too shy for society and too reserved for popularity, often unsympathetic and always seeming so, smothering emotions which he could not utter, schooled to universal distrust, stern to his followers and pitiless to himself, bearing the brunt of every hardship and danger, demanding of others an equal constancy joined to an implicit deference, heeding no counsel but his own, attempting the impossible and grasping what was too vast to hold.

But incomprehensible as it seems, for La Salle, his life, even with all its disappointments, was its own reward, and it is doubtful that even his gruesome death would have changed his opinion. Few men inspired such contradictory feelings on the part of their contemporaries; few men were so harshly judged, and so ill served by those that they had need to trust. Accordingly, let the last word be his: "The life I am leading has no other attraction for me than that of honor; and the more danger and difficulty there is in undertakings of this sort, the more worthy of honor I think they are." By those standards, it must all have been worthwhile.

AN

ACCOUNT

OF

Monſieur *de la* S A L L E's

LAST

Expedition and DISCOVERIES

IN

North *AMERICA.*

Preſented to the *French* King,

And Publiſhed by the

Chevalier *Tonti*, Governour of Fort St. *Louis*, in the Province of the *Iſlinois.*

Made *Engliſh* from the *Paris* Original.

ALSO

The ADVENTURES of the Sieur *de MONTAUBAN*, Captain of the French Buccaneers on the Coaſt of *Guinea*, in the Year **1695.**

LONDON

Printed for *J. Tonſon* at the *Judge's Head*, and *S. Buckley* at the *Dolphin* in *Fleet-ſtreet*, and *R. Knaplock*, at the *Angel* and *Grown* in St. *Paul's Church-Yard*. 1698.

The title page from an English-language edition of Tonti's account of La Salle's last expedition. After succeeding La Salle as governor of Fort St. Louis of Illinois, Tonti established the first European settlement on the lower Mississippi, at its confluence with the Arkansas.

Further Reading

Bald, F. Clever. *Michigan in Four Centuries*. New York: Harper and Brothers, 1954.

Caruso, John Anthony. *The Mississippi Valley Frontier: The Age of French Exploration and Settlement*. Indianapolis, IN: Bobbs-Merrill, 1966.

Delanglez, Jean. *Frontenac and the Jesuits*. Chicago: Institute of Jesuit History, 1939.

———. *Life and Voyages of Louis Jolliet*. Chicago: Institute of Jesuit History, 1948.

———. *Some La Salle Journeys*. Chicago: Institute of Jesuit History, 1938.

De Voto, Bernard. *The Course of Empire*. New York: American Heritage, 1989.

Donnelly, Joseph P. *Jacques Marquette*. Chicago: Loyola University Press, 1968.

Giraud, Marcel. *A History of French Louisiana*, Vol. I. Baton Rouge: Louisiana State University Press, 1974.

Gough, Barry. *Canada*. Englewood Cliffs, NJ: Prentice-Hall, 1973.

Hamilton, Raphael N. *Father Marquette*. Grand Rapids, MI: William B. Eerdmans, 1970.

———. *Marquette's Explorations: The Narratives Reexamined*. Madison: University of Wisconsin Press, 1970.

Jacobs, W. J. *Robert Cavelier de La Salle*. New York: Franklin Watts, 1975.

Josephy, Alvin M., Jr. *The Indian Heritage of America*. New York: Knopf, 1968.

Joutel, Henri. *A Journal of La Salle's Last Voyage.* New York: Corinth Books, 1962.

Madson, John. *Up on the River.* New York: Schocken Books, 1985.

Osler, E. B. *La Salle.* Toronto, Ont.: Longmans Canada, 1967.

Parkman, Francis. *The Discovery of the Great West: La Salle.* New York: Rinehart, 1956.

Terrell, John Upton. *La Salle: The Life and Times of an Explorer.* New York: Weybright and Talley, 1968.

Weddle, Robert S. *La Salle, the Mississippi, and the Gulf.* College Station: Texas A&M University Press, 1987.

———. *Wilderness Manhunt: The Spanish Search for La Salle.* Austin: University of Texas Press, 1973.

Chronology

Entries in roman type refer directly to La Salle and the exploration of the Mississippi; entries in italics refer to important historical and cultural events of the era.

1605–35	*Champlain founds settlements at Nova Scotia and Quebec; French fur traders travel as far west as Wisconsin, giving France claim to the interior of the continent*
Nov. 21, 1643	René-Robert Cavelier born in Rouen, France
1660	Enrolls in the Collège Henri IV, a Jesuit school near Angers
1663	*King Louis XIV declares New France a French province*
1667	Cavelier leaves the Jesuits and sails for New France; begins calling himself La Salle
1667–68	*France at war with Spain*
1669	La Salle sets out on an unsuccessful attempt to explore the Ohio River
1670–72	Commissioned to travel the Mississippi in search of a passage to Mexico; it is speculated that he spends this time in the wilderness trading with the Indians instead; the Great Lakes region is claimed in the name of France; Louis Jolliet and Father Jacques Marquette are dispatched to beat the English to the Mississippi; they reach the mouth of the river in June 1672
1673–75	La Salle is commissioned to build a fort on the north shore of Lake Ontario
1677	Wins approval of the French crown for an expedition to search for the mouth of the Mississippi; his actual intent is to colonize the Illinois Valley and trade with the Indians directly

1679–80	The expedition finally gets under way but stalls on the St. Joseph River near present-day Peoria, Illinois, where Fort Crèvecœur is built; La Salle travels to Fort Frontenac to get help and to learn the whereabouts of his ship, the *Griffin*
1681–82	Mounts a second expedition, which reaches the mouth of the Mississippi; he claims the region in the name of Louis XIV
1683–85	Returns to France and dupes the king into approving another expedition down the Mississippi by presenting him with a doctored map of the river; the expedition fails to find the mouth of the river and winds up 400 miles east in Matagorda Bay, Texas
1686–87	La Salle makes several unsuccessful attempts to locate the Mississippi from Texas; mutineers kill La Salle near present-day Navasota, Texas

Index

Picture Credits

Archives National Quebec: p. 58; The Bettmann Archive: pp. 12, 22, 48, 50, 52, 59, 66, 70, 90, 105; Edward Howland Blashfield, the Minnesota State Capitol: p. 51; George Catlin, courtesy the National Gallery of Art, Paul Melon Collection, Washington, D.C.: pp. 64 *La Salle Crossing Lake Michigan on the Ice, December 1681.* (#1965.16.331), 74–75 *Launching of the* Griffin, *1697* and *La Salle Driving the First Bolt for the* Griffin, *January 25, 1679* (#1965.16.321 and #1965.16.319), 76–77 *La Salle's Party Feasted in the Illinois Village, January 1680* (#1965.16.325), 78–79 *Launching a Canoe—Nass River* and *La Salle Received in the Village of the Cenis* (#1965.16.216 and #1965.16.340), 80 *La Salle's Party Entering the Mississippi in Canoes, February 6, 1682* (#1965.16.332), 83 *La Salle Erecting a Cross and Taking Possession of the Land, March 1682* (#1965.16.335), 85 *La Salle Claiming Louisiana for France, April 9, 1682* (#1965.16.336); Jean Loup Charmet: p. 60; L. C. Earle, *Winter Quarters of Father Marquette*, Chicago Historical Society: p. 37; William Lamprecht, detail from *Père Marquette and the Indians*, Marquette University, collection of the Haggerty Museum of Art, Milwaukee, Wisconsin. Copyright 1990: p. 38; Vikki Leib (map): p. 15; Library of Congress: pp. 16, 41, 46, 86, 94, 95, 97, 102; McCord Museum of Canadian History, Montreal: p. 28; Marquette University: p. 43; National Archives of Canada: pp. 55, 62, 65, 69, 103; National Archives of Canada, Map Collection: pp. 42, 69; New York Public Library, Map Division, Astor, Lenox and Tilden Foundations: pp. 19, 20, 33, 44, 92, 99; Photographie Giraudon/Art Resource: p. 63; Howard Pyle, *La Salle Petitions the King for Permission to Explore the Mississippi*, February 1905 *Harper's Monthly*, courtesy of the Delaware Art Museum: p. 73; Roger-Viollet: pp. 23, 24, 27, 30, 56, 89, 93

Tony Coulter has an M.A. in history from Columbia University. He is the host of two New York radio programs and currently resides in Brooklyn, New York.

William H. Goetzmann holds the Jack S. Blanton, Sr., Chair in History at the University of Texas at Austin, where he has taught for many years. The author of numerous works on American history and exploration, he won the 1967 Pulitzer and Parkman prizes for his *Exploration and Empire: The Role of the Explorer and Scientist in the Winning of the American West, 1800–1900*. With his son William N. Goetzmann, he coauthored *The West of the Imagination*, which received the Carr P. Collins Award in 1986 from the Texas Institute of Letters. His documentary television series of the same name received a blue ribbon in the history category at the American Film and Video Festival held in New York City in 1987. A recent work, *New Lands, New Men: America and the Second Great Age of Discovery*, was published in 1986 to much critical acclaim.

Michael Collins served as command module pilot on the *Apollo 11* space mission, which landed his colleagues Neil Armstrong and Buzz Aldrin on the moon. A graduate of the United States Military Academy, Collins was named an astronaut in 1963. In 1966 he piloted the *Gemini 10* mission, during which he became the third American to walk in space. The author of several books on space exploration, Collins was director of the Smithsonian Institution's National Air and Space Museum from 1971 to 1978 and is a recipient of the Presidential Medal of Freedom.